COOKBOOK

**YOUR PERSONAL
PROGRAMME FOR
NUTRITIOUS &
DELICIOUS
GUILT-FREE
FOOD**

An Hachette UK Company
www.hachette.co.uk

First published in Great Britain in 2012 by Hamlyn,
a division of Octopus Publishing Group Ltd
Endeavour House
189 Shaftesbury Avenue
London WC2H 8JY
www.octopusbooks.co.uk

ISBN 978-0-600-62452-3

A CIP catalogue record for this book is available from the British
Library.

Colour reproduction in the UK
Printed and bound in Italy

10 9 8 7 6 5 4 3 2

All reasonable care has been taken in the preparation of this book,
but the information it contains is not meant to take the place
of medical care under the direct supervision of a doctor. Before
making any changes in your heath and fitness regime, always
consult a doctor. Any application of the ideas and information
contained in this book is at the reader's sole discretion and risk.
Neither the author nor the publisher will be responsible for any
injury, loss, damages, actions, proceedings, claims, demands,
expenses and costs (including legal costs or expenses) incurring in
any way arising out of following the plan in this book.

'The Biggest Loser' is produced by Shine Limited for ITV1 based
on the formate owned by Reveille LLC.

'The Biggest Loser' is a registered trademark of Shine Limited. All
rights reserved.

Note:

Serving sizes vary. Some dishes (such as ratatouille) are
impractical if made for one, and soup – for
instance – is great made in bulk and frozen. The number
of people each dish serves is noted at the top,
but the calories listed are always for just one portion.

Dietitian Faith Toogood
Trainers Rob Edmond and Charlotte Ord
General Editor Gill Paul
Recipes Kate Santon

Publishing Director Stephanie Jackson
Senior Editors Leanne Bryan, Alex Stetter
Deputy Art Director Yasia Williams-Leedham
Design Nicky Collings
Photographer William Reavell
Food Stylist Laura Fyfe
Food Stylist's Assistant Madeline Rix
Props Stylists Rachel Jukes, Isabel de Cordova
Production Manager Peter Hunt

Shine would like to thank:
John Gilbert, Maya Maraj, Simone Foots, Karen Smith, Jamie
Munro, Lisa Perrin, Tane Bellwood, Verity Sutton Barrow,
Alan Williams, Eva Lofvenberg, Wayne Davison, Louise Hutchinson,
Aaron Kidd, Ian Ormiston, Lou Plank, Ben Comboy, Will Vaughan
and Digby Lewis

Photographic credits
All photographs are by William Reavell, with the exception of
the following: pages 7, 20 and 22: Neil Genower, copyright Shine
TV Ltd/ITV; page 173: Getty Images/Sandra Arduini

Both metric and imperial measurements have been given in all
recipes. Use one set of measurements only, and not a mixture
of both. Standard level spoon measurements are used in all
recipes. All spoon measures are level, unless otherwise indicated.

1 tablespoon = one 15 ml spoon

1 teaspoon = one 5 ml spoon

Ovens should be preheated to the specified temperature – if using
a fan-assisted oven, follow the manufacturer's instructions for
adjusting the time and the temperature.

Medium eggs should be used unless otherwise stated. The
Department of Health advises that eggs should not be consumed
raw. This book contains some dishes made with raw or lightly
cooked eggs. It is prudent for vulnerable people such as pregnant
and nursing mothers, invalids, the elderly, babies and young
children to avoid uncooked or lightly cooked dishes made with
eggs. Once prepared, these dishes should be kept refrigerated and
used promptly.

This book includes dishes made with nuts and nut derivatives. It is
advisable for those with known allergic reactions to nuts and nut
derivatives and those who may be potentially vulnerable to these
allergies to avoid dishes made with nuts and nut oils. It is also
prudent to check the labels of pre-prepared ingredients for the
possible inclusion of nut derivatives.

Contents

Foreword

Faith Toogood, Biggest Loser dietitian

Congratulations! Whether you are in the middle of a weight-loss programme or just starting out, you are on track to make a real difference to your life.

Previous winners of the Biggest Loser TV series all talk about how much they hated being seen as a 'big girl' or 'big guy'. They may have disguised it with humour, but other people's negative attitudes hurt. One of the best things about getting down to a healthy weight is that people will see you as yourself, not as 'the fat person' – and that feels special.

The Biggest Loser Weight-Loss Programme is so successful because it is easy to follow and the foods you can choose are delicious and filling. Biggest Losers keep the weight off because they learn how to eat healthily – and exercise – for life. This is not a 'diet' and it is not about denying yourself your favourite foods. This is about making good choices, enjoying food and learning to cook healthy meals without compromising on flavour.

This cookbook has more than a hundred recipes that taste so good you'll never believe they're low calorie, and they're all so simple to make. There are healthy versions of family favourites, such as Steak with herby, healthy chips (see page 150), and there are some exotic dishes, such as Spicy North African prawns with rice (see page 126) and Moroccan lamb casserole with apricots (see page 144). There are desserts, healthy snacks and also a treats allowance so you can still have that glass of wine or chocolate bar.

There's no counting of calories – we've done it all for you. You can follow a two-week plan with a generous calorie allowance so you don't go hungry, or you can use the recipes to add a bit of spice to your menus if you are already following the Biggest Loser programme online or using one of the previous books.

You won't have to eat healthily for long before you start to feel amazing. You'll soon find you have more energy as the pounds start to drop off and the compliments start flooding in. Your digestion will work more efficiently, your clothes will fit better, and you should feel very proud of your achievement when you weigh yourself each week. We're proud of you!

Set yourself a clear goal at the beginning of your weight-loss journey, or if you have already started, reset your goals if you have lost sight of them. Focus and allow yourself to move forwards.

Enjoy the recipes in this book – and enjoy the new slim you that is about to be revealed!

Introduction

It is possible to be overweight because you eat too much healthy food – but in our experience fat people are fat because they eat too much junk. What do we mean by junk? They are foods that are not only high in calories and fat, but also provide few (if any) of the proteins, vitamins and minerals we need for good health.

The first step on any weight-loss programme is to cut right back on these 'empty' calories. That means limiting your intake of:

• sugar

• sweets and chocolate

• cakes and biscuits

• pastries and pies

• crisps

• deep-fried foods

• oily takeaways, such as pizza, fish and chips, burgers and curries

• ice cream

• desserts with whipped cream and custard

• alcohol

Does that sound like your staple diet? If so, you've got some BIG changes to make.

The most important rule on the Biggest Loser Weight-Loss Plan is to eat fresh, healthy foods, and learn how to prepare them yourself.

That way, you can avoid all the fattening additives that are routinely added to shop-bought products. It may take a little time to cook for yourself but the benefits to your health will be enormous. Besides, it's almost always cheaper to make your own food, and if you cook meals for a partner or family you'll be boosting their health as well.

Think you can't cook? You haven't tried our Biggest Loser recipes. They're straightforward and foolproof, with no fancy equipment or mysterious chefs' techniques. If you can boil a kettle and make a cup of coffee, we guarantee you'll manage these recipes just fine.

Now we're not saying that you should sprout wings and become a saint in order to lose weight. If you denied yourself all your favourite foods, your halo would slip before long. That's why we give you a daily 'treats' allowance, so that you can still have a pint with your mates, or a couple of squares of chocolate while watching the TV. What's more, you'll be able to choose your own treats, so long as they fall within your daily allowance (see page 13 for more on this).

There's a two-week menu plan on pages 16–19 to get you started, but once you understand the way the Biggest Loser Weight-loss Programme works, you can mix and match the recipes in this book to suit yourself. We want you to get used to eating healthily for life, not just for two weeks – so that you keep your brand new figure and enjoy the new you!

Our Top 10 Biggest Loser Guidelines

1 Buy food in as natural a state as you can – fresh fruit and vegetables rather than canned; raw chicken, fish and lean meat, rather than pre-cooked in a sauce. That way, when you cook meals yourself, you'll know exactly what's gone into them.

2 Choose low-fat options whenever there's a choice: skimmed milk, low-fat spread for bread, light mayonnaise, 0% fat yogurt and low-fat crème fraîche. Remove the skin from chicken and cut visible fat off meat before cooking. It makes a huge difference to the calorie content of a meal.

3 Buy a set of scales and measures, and stick to the quantities given in recipes. It's easy to be over-generous, particularly with the more fattening ingredients, such as cheese and oil, but you will have to be strict if you want to see results on the scales.

4 Buy non-stick pans so you can use minimum quantities of oil for cooking. Just 1 tablespoon of cooking oil has 120 calories while 1 teaspoon has only 40 – but a 'glug' can have several hundred.

5 Don't be tempted to skip meals. Your blood sugar levels will drop, causing cravings for sweet, stodgy foods that can be hard to resist. And if you keep starving yourself, you could find your metabolism slows down so it gets harder to burn off calories.

6 Remove temptation from your kitchen. If you don't have cakes and biscuits in the cupboard or ice cream in the freezer, you're less likely to succumb to late-night munchies.

7 Don't cut whole food groups, such as carbs, or you'll make yourself unhealthy in the long run. Try to include some fruit and vegetables, protein, carb and a little fat in every meal.

8 Plan meals and shop in advance so you can be sure you have all the ingredients to hand. The shopping list on page 19 will help.

9 Write down everything you eat and drink in a food diary. It's a useful nudge to your conscience. You're less likely to gobble the kids' jelly snakes if you have to confess in black and white afterwards!

10 And don't forget your daily treat! It's psychologically important to have a little indulgence to look forward to. See pages 169–172 for tips on choosing your treat.

How Much Do You Need to Lose?

You may think you know how much weight you should be shedding, even if you've been avoiding the scales since the pounds started to creep on – but in our experience a lot of people badly underestimate their own weight, so you could be in for a shock. Brace yourself!

It's easy to ignore an expanding waistline if you tend to buy loose, stretchy trousers or skirts and team them with baggy shirts.

One tip for keeping an eye on your weight long-term is to wear fitted clothes with snug waistbands, so you get an instant wake-up call when it's a struggle to fasten the top button.

Doctors recommend that we aim at a weight for our height that gives us a healthy score on the BMI (body mass index) chart. That's the weight at which your heart will work most efficiently and your risk of getting life-threatening diseases will be lowest. Slipping into the 'obese' or 'morbidly obese' categories may well shorten your life – but getting back to a healthy BMI boosts your chances of living to a ripe old age.

Reading the chart

Find your height on the BMI chart opposite. Now run your finger along the horizontal line beside it until you are within the band marked 'healthy'. Follow an intersecting line up to the top of the chart and you'll see the weight you should be in kilos. If you prefer to work in stones and pounds, run your finger down to the bottom of the chart. So, for example, if you are 5 foot 7 inches tall, you'll see in the chart opposite that your weight should be between 56 and 70 kilos (roughly 9 to 11 stone).

Now for the moment of truth …

1 Step on the scales and find out what you weigh.

2 Now calculate the difference between that weight and what you should weigh to have a healthy BMI. That's how much you need to lose. Gulp!

3 Now look at your current weight on the chart. With your finger, follow the vertical line down to the bottom where you will see shaded areas marked with letters of the alphabet. If you are female, look at the upper area. Are you an A, B, C or D? If you are male, look at the lower area and work out if you fall into category B, C or D. These are important, because they will determine the menu plan you will follow to help you shed the excess flab and get yourself right back to a healthy BMI – and a fantastic new figure!

BMI Chart

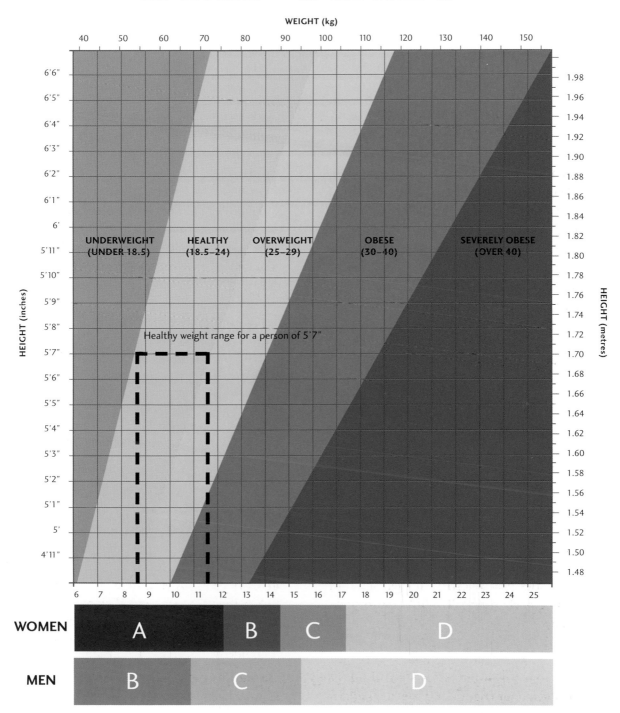

WEIGHT (kg)

UNDERWEIGHT (UNDER 18.5)   HEALTHY (18.5–24)   OVERWEIGHT (25–29)   OBESE (30–40)   SEVERELY OBESE (OVER 40)

Healthy weight range for a person of 5'7"

HEIGHT (inches)   **HEIGHT (metres)**

WOMEN   A   B   C   D

MEN   B   C   D

Setting Realistic Targets

In modern society we're programmed to expect a quick fix for everything, which is why so-called crash diets occasionally top the bestseller lists – until users find out that any initial weight loss is swiftly followed by an even greater weight gain as the body adjusts its internal mechanisms, or until hunger drives you to binge-eat.

This book offers a long-term plan for sustained, healthy weight loss. We recommend that you break down your goals into manageable chunks and give each chunk a deadline. It's a good idea to target forthcoming events. If there's a school reunion coming up, or a wedding, work out how many weeks there are until the date and set your goal accordingly. For example, if it's 10 weeks away, aim to lose 10 kilos or 20 pounds by the big day. Once you've achieved that, set another goal with a new target.

Don't jump on the scales every time you're passing. Sometimes, despite your best efforts, you might fail to lose weight on a particular day. You might even gain a pound or two. There are all sorts of reasons why this can happen, so don't feel disheartened. If you are following our weight-loss plan carefully, you should lose some weight every week, and that's why we recommend only weighing yourself once a week.

Step on the scales at the same time of day each week, either naked or wearing the same clothing, and jot down the results in a little weight-loss diary. Watching the numbers drop is a good way of staying motivated. Keep wearing fitted clothes during the daytime, and pat yourself on the back as the waistbands get looser. It's always a special moment when you realise you can fit into a whole size smaller than you wore before.

Do it with friends

A weight-loss buddy is a great tool for success. If it's your partner, you can take turns to cook meals and discourage each other from walking down the dessert aisle in the supermarket. If it's a friend, you can still get together for exercise sessions and weigh-ins or offer encouragement by phone. Tell friends and relatives that you are on a weight-loss programme and ask them not to tempt you with home baking or gin and tonics. They'll be proud as they see the new, healthier you emerging – and that should make you even more determined to achieve your target weight.

How the Plan Works

The meal plans on pages 16–17 are carefully calculated so that you will have plenty to eat and won't feel hungry but will still lose weight.

If you are following Plan A, which provides 1,500 calories a day, you should prepare the quantities shown in the recipes and eat just one portion. Those on Plans B, C or D eat the same basic meals as those on Plan A, but they can also have some extras, which are listed underneath each recipe. Plan B has a total of 2,000 calories day, Plan C has a total of 2,500 and Plan D has a total of 3,000.

Those who are heavier are allowed to eat more because they need more calories for their bodies to carry out essential functions, such as breathing and blood circulation. If a 30-stone man tried to follow Plan A, he would feel weak, dizzy and starving, and wouldn't stay the course. As the weight drops off, those on Plan D are promoted to C, then to B, and women should eventually reach Plan A.

Look at the BMI chart on page 11 to find out the weight at which you will be ready to progress to the next level. As it approaches, you can start to reduce the number of extras you eat so that when the time comes the switch feels effortless.

You don't have to eat your extras at each meal if you're not hungry, but always carry a healthy snack with you so you don't get tempted by junk food between meals. Healthy snacks are listed on pages 169, and you can choose your favourites, or the ones that fit in with your lifestyle, so long as you stick to the snack quota for the day shown in the right-hand column of the meal plans on pages 16–17.

Note that your snacks allowance is for healthy snacks only. Don't confuse this with the treats allowance, which is quite separate. Treats are naughty but nice. They're good for morale, if not for the waistline.

Your treat allowance

- Those on Plan **A** can have a 100-calorie treat per day.
- Those on Plan **B** can have a 150-calorie treat per day.
- Those on Plan **C** can have a 200-calorie treat per day.
- Those on Plan **D** can have a 250-calorie treat per day.

Your treat allowance can be used for an alcoholic drink, some sweets, a cake or crisps, ice cream or pudding – whatever your favourite indulgence might be.

Cheats & Swaps

You might be surprised to hear that we encourage cheating on the Biggest Loser Weight Loss Plan – well, a certain kind of cheating, at least. If you can get all the flavour of a food or drink with only half the calories, why on earth wouldn't you? And if you can slash the calorie content of a meal simply by using a different cooking method, you'd mad not to. On these pages, we're sharing some of our favourite cheats and swaps, because at the end of the day we want you all to become Biggest Losers!

Choose healthy cooking methods

Frying adds fat to your food, and deep-frying adds most of all. Grilling, boiling, baking, steaming, poaching and microwaving are the healthiest cooking methods. Stir-frying is fine if you use minimal oil and keep the food moving around in a very hot wok so it cooks quickly.

Adapt your recipes

There's no need to give up family favourites such as shepherd's pie, lasagne or apple pie for the rest of your life. Make recipes healthier and lower in calories by cutting down on the amount of fat and sugar in them: use lean meat, low-fat dairy and less oil, then include extra vegetables or pulses; add sweetness to puddings with ripe fruit rather than sugar.

Use a smaller plate/glass

If you currently serve your main meal on a plate that is, say, 27 cm (10½ inches) across, try switching to one that is 24 cm (9½ inches). Swap a 250 ml (8 fl oz) glass for a 175 ml (6 fl oz) one. Research shows you'll feel satisfied after eating or drinking less if your plate or glass is full.

Eat before you shop

This is a well-known tip but we're repeating it here because it makes a massive difference. If you go to the supermarket starving, you'll be much more likely to slip sugary, fatty items into your basket, almost without noticing it. 'How did these doughnuts get in here? Oh well, suppose I'd better not let them go to waste …'

Drink lots of water

If you feel hungry, try drinking a big glass of water (zero calories) rather than snacking on a choccie biccie (lots of calories). Water fills you up and decreases the appetite.

Exercise!

We're not going to bang on about exercise in this book, but you all know that it is a vital part of any weight-loss programme. The more muscle you have, the more calories you burn and the more weight you lose. That's why we've included exercise as a 'cheat'.

Keep healthy snacks nearby

There are plenty to choose from on page 169. Make sure you always have some in the fridge, in your desk at the office, in the car, or in your briefcase or handbag if you move around a lot. That way, you've got no excuse for a trip to the vending machine.

Virtually Painless Swaps

SWAP THIS ...

FOR THIS

1 tablespoon butter (111 calories) ⟶ 1 tablespoon low-fat spread (52 calories)

20 g (¾ oz) Cheddar cheese (84 calories) ⟶ 20 g (¾ oz) Feta cheese (50 calories)

100 g (3½ oz) roasted chicken breast, with skin (171 calories) ⟶ 100 g (3½ oz) roasted skinless chicken breast (115 calories)

175 g (6 oz) deep-fried chips (490 calories) ⟶ 175 g (6 oz) our Herby, healthy chips, see page 150 (170 calories)

35 g (1¼ oz) bag crisps (184 calories) ⟶ air-popped popcorn, no added butter (130 calories)

Takeaway chicken tikka masala with pilau rice (about 1000 calories) ⟶ our Chicken Curry with boiled rice, see page 134 (420–450 calories)

1 tablespoon double cream (75 calories) ⟶ 1 tablespoon half-fat crème fraiche (25 calories)

1 average Danish pastry (430 calories) ⟶ 1 slice of wholemeal toast with low-fat spread and 1 teaspoon jam (125 calories)

100 g (3½ oz) fish, deep-fried in batter (247 calories) ⟶ 100 g (3½ oz) grilled fish without batter (95 calories)

a tall latte made with whole milk (176 calories) ⟶ a tall latte made with skimmed milk (102 calories)

1 tablespoon full-fat mayonnaise (105 calories) ⟶ 1 tablespoon fat-free salad dressing (10 calories)

a 250 ml (8 fl oz) glass of whole milk (165 calories) ⟶ a 250 ml (8 fl oz) glass of skimmed milk (80 calories)

1 teaspoon peanut butter (30 calories) ⟶ 1 teaspoon Marmite (9 calories)

100 g (3½ oz) egg-fried rice (200 calories) ⟶ 100 g (3½ oz) plain boiled rice (138 calories)

an average portion Spaghetti Bolognese (720 calories) ⟶ our Pasta with tomatoes and chillies, see page 66 (465 calories)

tea with whole milk and 2 teaspoons sugar (46 calories) ⟶ tea with skimmed milk and no sugar (8 calories)

(40 g/1½ oz) tortilla chips and sour cream dip (230 calories) ⟶ crudités and Herb salsa, see page 42 (160 calories)

1 tablespoon balsamic vinegar (15 calories) ⟶ 1 tablespoon wine vinegar (3 calories)

125 g (4 oz) pot whole-milk strawberry yogurt (131 calories) ⟶ 125 g (4 oz) low-fat strawberry yogurt (112 calories)

Your Biggest Loser Meal Plan

Week one

	Monday	Tuesday	Wednesday	Thursday	Friday	Saturday	Sunday
Breakfast	Porridge with dried fruit & yogurt (see page 29)	Breakfast bagel (see page 35)	Breakfast fruit glory (see page 32)	Cheese omelette (see page 37)	Start-the-day smoothie and toast (see page 26)	Scrambled eggs & smoked salmon (see page 38)	Baked eggs & wholemeal toast (see page 37)
Lunch	Carrot & red pepper soup (see page 82) Spinach, smoky bacon & poached egg salad (see page 75)	Tomato & coriander soup with yogurt (see page 82) Feta cheese & lentil salad (see page 47)	Paprika mushrooms on toast with a great big salad (see page 77) B,C,D ONLY Black bean soup with celery (see page 95)	Italian bread & tomato salad (see page 44) B,C,D ONLY Black bean soup with celery (see page 95)	Vegetable couscous with tomato & chilli sauce (see page 72)	Warm chickpea, beetroot & onion salad (see page 55) C, D ONLY Watercress soup (see page 88)	Pear, blue cheese & walnut salad (see page 52) C, D ONLY Sweet potato and sweetcorn soup (see page 85)
Dinner	Chicken curry with yogurt (see page 138) Golden fruit salad with cinnamon and vanilla (see page 157)	Tuna with Mexican salsa (see page 116) C,D ONLY Fruit kebabs (see page 163)	Steak with herby, healthy chips (see page 150) Strawberry ice (see page 154)	Spicy North African Prawns with rice (see page 126) Baked apple with fruit & nuts (see page 166)	Baked cod with a crispy tomato crust (see page 118) Vanilla rhubarb with honey & ice cream (see page 164)	Moroccan lamb casserole with apricots (see page 144) Nectarines in wine (see page 160)	Chicken with olives, lemon & chickpeas (see page 135) Orange with toasted pine nuts, honey & yogurt (see page 154)
Snacks	A: 50 kCals B: 150 kCals C: 300 kCals D: 450 kCals	A: 50 kCals B: 150 kCals C: 50 kCals D: 200 kCals	A: 50 kCals B: 150 kCals C: 450 kCals D: 550 kCals	A: 150 kCals B: 150 kCals C: 250 kCals D: 250 kCals	A: 50 kCals B: 100 kCals C: 300 kCals D: 350 kCals	A: 100 kCals B: 300 kCals C: 100 kCals D: 200 kCals	A: 50 kCals B: 200 kCals C: 200 kCals D: 300 kCals

• Those on Plans B, C and D will find the extras they can have listed at the end of each recipe.

• Choose your healthy snacks from the list on page 169, making sure you don't have more than the calories allowed for your plan on each day (the snack allowance for each meal plan is listed in the Snacks column below – be aware that it changes daily according to the recipe suggestions from the rest of each day).

• On top of this you can have your daily treat (see pages 171–172).

Week two

	Monday	Tuesday	Wednesday	Thursday	Friday	Saturday	Sunday
Breakfast	Mango & citrus salad (see page 30)	Wholegrain muesli (see page 29)	Hot fruit salad with orange juice (see page 30)	Porridge with dried fruit & yogurt (see page 29)	Breakfast fruit glory (see page 32)	Scrambled eggs & smoked salmon (see page 38)	Cheese omelette (see page 37)
Lunch	Beetroot soup with yogurt (see page 90) Black-eyed bean salad (see page 61)	Grilled goats' cheese on a bed of rocket (see page 48)	Pasta with tomatoes & chillies (see page 66)	Greek bean stew (see page 104) C, D only: Greek summer salad (see page 50)	Baked potatoes three ways (see page 70) B, C, D, only: Vanilla rhubarb with honey & ice cream (see page 164)	Cauliflower cheese with smoky bacon (see page 67)	Dhal with chapatti and raita (see page 98) C, D only: Warm pear compôte (see page 166)
Dinner	Salmon fillets with pesto & pasta (see page 123) C, D only: Warm pear compôte (see page 166)	Chicken, bacon & mushroom stew (see page 106) B, C, D only: Dried apricot fool (see page 160)	Steak with herby, healthy chips (see page 150)	Grilled plaice with lemon & orange sauce & new potatoes (see page 124) Baked apple with fruit & nuts (see page 166)	Refreshing Chinese vegetable soup with prawns (see page 96) Stir-fried chicken with mangetout or green beans (see page 133)	Lamb cutlet with chickpeas, shallots & parsley (see page 143) B, C, D only: Golden fruit salad (see page 157)	Tunisian fish stew with couscous (see page 106) Orange with toasted pine nuts, honey & yogurt (see page 158)
Snacks	A: 50 kCals B: 200 kCals C: 50 kCals D: 250 kCals	A: 150 kCals B: 50 kCals C: 150 kCals D: 250 kCals	A: 150 kCals B: 50 kCals C: 150 kCals D: 250 kCals	A: 200 kCals B: 300 kCals C: 50 kCals D: 200 kCals	A: 100 kCals B: 50 kCals C: 300 kCals D: 450 kCals	A: 100 kCals B: 100 kCals C: 200 kCals D: 350 kCals	A: 50 kCals B: 150 kCals C: 150 kCals D: 350 kCals

Get Ready to Start Losing

Don't choose a starting date that's just days before a big family wedding or during a particularly stressful period at work. You could find yourself making excuses to slip off track, then it's hard to get back on again. On the other hand, don't leave it too long before starting. The slim new you is waiting to be revealed.

Make sure you have everything you need lined up and ready to go.

Clear the junk food from your cupboards – apart from any items you want to keep for your daily treats – then start buying the food you'll need for the two-week menu plan (see opposite). Stock up on the storecupboard items at the outset, but plan to buy your fruit, veg, fish and meat fresh every few days, as and when you need it.

Buy a notebook in which to record your decreasing weight every week and write down all the food you eat (and all the drinks you drink, apart from water).

If you don't have any bathroom scales, it's time to buy some. It's up to you whether you want a fancy set that shows your body-fat percentage, or just a basic one with kilos and pounds.

You'll need a measuring jug and a set of measuring spoons, plus an accurate set of kitchen scales to weigh your food.

If you want to choose your own foods after finishing the two-week menu plan, you'll need a calorie counter. Buy a small book, find a calorie-counting website or get a mobile phone app.

Decide on the exercise regime you will follow and make sure you have all the equipment you'll need for it.

Stick to your weight-loss shopping list opposite and stock up with healthy foods.

Your before and after photos

It's a great idea to remind yourself why you are on a weight-loss programme by taking some pictures before you start. Be brutal. Get a sideways view that shows how far that belly sticks out. Take a picture of yourself in underwear or swimwear, displaying all those unsightly bulges. You needn't show the pictures to anyone else if you don't want to – just stick them in your weight-loss notebook as a reminder – but you might find that once you reach your target weight you will be so proud of your achievement you'll want to show the world.

Your weight-loss shopping list

Fruit and vegetables

Bananas, apples, pears
Strawberries, raspberries, blueberries
Pink grapefruit
Lemons, oranges, limes
Mango, kiwis, canteloupe melon
Victoria plums, peaches, nectarines
Rhubarb
Tomatoes, cherry tomatoes
Celery, cucumber
Fresh basil, chives, parsley, mint, thyme, coriander, rosemary
Spring onions
Red onions, white onions, shallots
Red and green chillis
Peppers: green and red
Salad leaves: plain ones like Cos, and sharper ones, such as rocket
Spinach leaves, watercress
Garlic, root ginger
Cabbage, black kale
Carrots
Cauliflower
Baby beetroot, medium beetroot
Butternut squash
Sweet potatoes
Aubergines, courgettes
Potatoes, new potatoes
Leeks
Pak choi, or Chinese leaves
Mangetout or French beans
Purple sprouting broccoli
Button mushrooms (or your favourite types of mushroom)

Meat and fish

Smoked salmon
Cooked prawns (normal size and king prawns)
Monkfish tail (or cod)
Cod loins
Haddock fillets
Salmon fillets
Plaice fillets
Tuna steaks
Chicken breasts, skinless
Streaky bacon, back bacon
Lamb cutlets or chops
Diced lamb, or lamb leg steaks
Pork fillets
Extra-lean minced beef
Fillet steaks

Foods for the fridge

Skimmed or semi-skimmed milk
Single cream, low-fat crème fraîche
Low-fat natural yogurt
Low-fat Greek yogurt
Fresh orange juice, apple juice
Low-fat spread
Butter
Eggs
Light cream cheese, cottage cheese
Cheddar cheese, or your favourite type of cheese
Feta cheese, Parmesan
Roquefort, or any blue cheese
Goats' cheese log
Light mayonnaise
Light soy sauce
Wholegrain mustard, French mustard
Sweet chilli dipping sauce
Tomato purée
Chutney
Fresh chicken stock
Sun-dried tomatoes in oil
Harissa paste (optional)

For the freezer

Frozen broad beans
Frozen peas
Vanilla ice cream, low-fat

Foods for the storecupboard

Olive oil, sunflower or rapeseed oil, sesame oil
Sugar, caster sugar, Demerara sugar
Plain flour, wholemeal flour
Clear, runny honey
Smooth peanut butter
Black olives in brine
Vegetable stock cubes, or granules
Chicken stock cubes, or granules
Balsamic, white wine & cider vinegar
Peanut butter, jam or marmalade (your choice)
Marmite (if you like it)
Whole porridge oats (not instant oats)
Sultanas, raisins, dried apricots, dates, prunes
Desiccated coconut
Whole nuts: almonds, hazelnuts, walnuts
Pistachio nuts and monkey nuts in their shells
Flaked almonds
Crispbread, oatcakes
Sesame seeds
Pine nuts
Lentils (preferably Puy), dried
Red lentils, or yellow split peas, dried
Black-eyed beans, dried or canned
Black beans, dried
Borlotti beans, canned
Butter beans, canned
Kidney beans, canned
Chickpeas, canned
Couscous
Rice, long-grain, basmati and risotto rice (arborio)
Pasta: penne and wholewheat spaghetti
Cans of chopped tomatoes
Cans of sweetcorn
Cans of tuna in spring water
Sardines in spring water
Cans of baked beans (if liked)
Cans of light coconut milk
Jars of pesto
Brandy snap biscuits
Sponge fingers
Ice-cream fan wafers

Spice rack

Black pepper, white pepper, cayenne pepper, salt
Mixed dried herbs (herbs de Provence if you like)
Dried thyme
Dried bay leaves
Paprika, chilli powder
Ground cumin, ground coriander
Turmeric, garam masala
Cajun spice mix
Dried ginger
Dried cinnamon, cinnamon sticks
Vanilla essence
Orange-flower water
Cloves

Bread bin

Granary or wholemeal bread (you can have rolls on Plan D)
Plain bagels (you can have seeded ones if you are on Plans C or D)
Ciabatta bread (or ciabatta rolls)
Wholemeal pitta breads

Drinks

Herbal teas
Fruit juices (these are quite high in calories, so only have them as 'extras' or 'healthy snacks')
Your normal tea and coffee (try to cut the sugar, if you can; if you can't, it will have to come out of your treats allowance, at 20 calories per teaspoon)
Red wine (for cooking)
Rosé wine (used for Nectarines in wine, see page 160)
Whisky (if you like – used in Scottish cream, see page 157)
Any alcoholic drinks you want to have as a treat

Top Tips
From trainer Rob Edmond

I believe in having a life. Sometimes I eat foods that may not be the best for me and I'm not a teetotaller, but I eat and drink in moderation – that's the key. When I'm working with clients who want to lose weight I suggest they chip away at their bad habits one by one rather than trying to change everything all at once.

First of all, I tell them to look at their portion sizes. I know children are encouraged from an early age to eat everything on their plates, but you're an adult now, so break the habit. When a plate of food is brought to you in a restaurant or while you're out socialising, just eat until you feel full. Even if it's the best meal in the world, don't stuff yourself. At home, get rid of your oversized plates – throw them out! – and get some smaller ones.

My favourite food is curry, with lots of ginger, chillies, spices and a good meat, such as chicken. Hot food that makes you sweat can actually speed up the metabolism. If you like spice, make your own curries or chilli dishes. I have three or four curries a week.

Once you've got your portion sizes down and you've started cooking healthy food for yourself, try to give your body a break by 'eating clean' one day a week. By this I mean having a whole day with no processed foods or drinks containing preservatives, colourings or other additives. This would include shop-bought bread, fizzy drinks, alcohol, jarred sauces and so forth. Use only natural products to give your body a break. Some of your fat stores actually lock in toxins to protect your body from them, so when you cut out toxins, the fat can be released. Start with one 'clean' day a week, then increase it to two, then three or more in a row, as this gives your body a real break from them.

You might lose weight if you cut down on your food intake without exercising, but aside from the other benefits of exercise, you will also lose your muscle mass, as the body will eat away at your muscles before the fat. Your muscles are your engine, and it's harder to burn off fuel from the fat stores if your engine is smaller, as it requires less fuel. This is why crash diets don't work, as once you inevitably resume normal eating, you'll put more fat back on quicker because your engine requires less fuel to run it and the excess gets stored as fat.

Human beings have been around a long time but the Western diet of high-sugar, processed foods, and the Western lifestyle of sitting at computers and driving everywhere in cars, are relatively recent. We used to work hard to collect our food, through hunting and gathering, and that's what our bodies are designed for. To stay healthy, we need to get enough exercise to keep our heart muscle strong and our bodies fit. Keep those engines firing!

The Next Level

Top Tips
From trainer Charlotte Ord

I am very careful with my own diet, because as a trainer I need to keep myself lean. I have a home-cooked meal every day and eat plenty of lean protein and vegetables. I recommend that you eat something every two to three hours, so you never let hunger build up. Eat lean protein and veg at every meal, but save starchy carbs such as bread, rice and pasta for after a work-out when the glycogen is depleted. Make sure you have some healthy fats every day as well: using olive oil for salad dressings and rapeseed oil for cooking is a good start.

Usually by the time people come to see me for help with weight loss, they feel helpless and don't have a good self-image. The way to turn this around is to design a programme that lets them see results happening in stages – like a road map for success – and that's what I suggest you do at home. You wouldn't set off on any long journey without a map, and you need one for your weight-loss journey as well.

Break your overall goals down into small sub-goals: for example, aim to lose two pounds in a week, eight pounds in a month. Take your waist measurement and check it every week at the same time as you weigh in, because once you start building muscle you'll be losing fat in that all-important abdominal area. Note your body-fat percentage as well if you have access to scales that show this. Every little improvement you see will help to boost your motivation.

When it comes to your exercise programme, it's a good idea to get a trainer to design one for you, if possible, because we all have individual needs. Make sure your exercise routine combines strength training with interval training. Ideally you should be aiming to get five or six hours of exercise a week – roughly an hour a day, with one day off. Change your exercise programme as your body begins to adapt and you start finding it easier. Don't get stuck in a rut but keep ringing the changes and challenging yourself for best results.

I believe that the odd scheduled splurge is no bad thing. Don't deny yourself a meal out on a special occasion, but stick to healthy eating for the rest of the week and it shouldn't set you back. It could even give your metabolism a boost! But don't splurge too often … once a week is enough when you're trying to lose weight.

Keep taking small steps towards your goal and you may well get there sooner than you think. Go on – you can do it!

Breakfast

Start-the-day smoothie 26

Raspberry vanilla smoothie 26

Porridge with dried fruit & yogurt 29

Wholegrain muesli 29

Mango & citrus salad 30

Hot fruit salad with orange juice 30

Breakfast fruit glory 32

Breakfast bagels 35

Baked eggs & wholemeal toast 37

Cheese omelette 37

Scrambled eggs & smoked salmon 38

Start-the-day smoothie

CALORIES PER PORTION 220 kCals, plus 100 if serving with granary toast and low-fat spread

Smoothies are simple to prepare and a great way to wake up your taste buds. Choose the flavour you prefer, and serve with a slice of granary toast and low-fat spread.

SERVES 1   1 SMALL BANANA, VERY RIPE, PEELED AND CHOPPED | 50 G (2 OZ) RIPE STRAWBERRIES, HULLED AND CHOPPED
100 ML (3½ FL OZ) SEMI-SKIMMED MILK | 2 TABLESPOONS FRESH ORANGE JUICE
4 TABLESPOONS LOW-FAT NATURAL YOGURT | 1 TEASPOON HONEY

SERVE WITH: A SLICE OF GRANARY TOAST WITH 1 TEASPOON LOW-FAT SPREAD

1. Put the fruit in a food processor or blender and add the milk, juice, yogurt and honey. Blend until smooth and check the texture; if you like it more liquid, add a little water and blend again.

2. Pour the smoothie into a container and chill in the fridge for 10 minutes. Add an ice cube if you wish. Once it is cool, have it with a slice of granary toast and low-fat spread.

B Have your smoothie with an extra slice of granary toast with 1 teaspoon low-fat spread (this adds 100 calories)

C Have your smoothie with a 40 g (1½ oz) bowl of high-fibre, unsweetened cereal (i.e. without chocolate, sugar or honey) served with 100 ml (3½ fl oz) skimmed milk (this adds 200 calories)

D Have your smoothie with a bowl of cereal, as for C, as well as the granary toast, as for B (this adds 300 calories)

Raspberry vanilla smoothie

CALORIES PER PORTION 175 kCals, plus 25 if the honey is used and 100 if serving with granary toast and low-fat spread

SERVES 1   125 G (4 OZ) RASPBERRIES | 150 G (5 OZ) LOW-FAT NATURAL YOGURT | 2 DROPS VANILLA ESSENCE
1 TEASPOON CLEAR HONEY (OPTIONAL) | 1 HEAPED TABLESPOON LOW-FAT GREEK YOGURT

SERVE WITH: A SLICE OF GRANARY TOAST WITH LOW-FAT SPREAD

1. Put the raspberries, yogurt and vanilla essence in a food processor or blender and blend until smooth. Taste, and add the honey if necessary for sweetness.

2. Put a couple of ice cubes in a glass, and pour in the smoothie. Spoon the Greek yogurt on top, add a straw and serve immediately.

Porridge with dried fruit & yogurt

CALORIES PER PORTION 250 kCals

Porridge is the dieter's friend, with slow-release carbs that will keep you feeling full right through the morning.

SERVES 1 35G (1½ OZ) PORRIDGE OATS | 1 HEAPED TABLESPOON SULTANAS | 4 SMALL DRIED APRICOTS, QUARTERED 250 ML (8 FL OZ) WATER | 1 HEAPED TABLESPOON LOW-FAT GREEK YOGURT

1. Put the porridge oats in a non-stick saucepan and add most of the sultanas and 3 apricots. Cover with water and place over a medium heat.

2. After about 5 minutes the porridge will start to bubble; stir it well and keep an eye on it as it cooks and thickens. When it has reached the consistency you like, pour it into a bowl, scatter the reserved sultanas and apricot on top and spoon the yogurt on the side. Serve immediately.

B Have your porridge with a fruit salad of 1 medium chopped apple and 1 small chopped pear (this adds 115 calories)

C Have a fruit salad, as for B, and a slice of wholemeal toast with 1 teaspoon low-fat spread and 1 teaspoon peanut butter or jam as well (this adds 240–245 calories)

D Have a fruit salad, as for B, and add 2 slices of wholemeal toast with low-fat spread and peanut butter or jam, as for C (this adds 365–375 calories)

Wholegrain muesli

CALORIES PER PORTION 360 kCals

A hundred times better than shop-bought muesli, this is naturally sweet, with a satisfying mix of textures. This recipe needs to be started the night before to allow time for soaking the porridge oats and sultanas.

SERVES 2 75 g (3 oz) jumbo porridge oats (whole oats, not instant) | 25 G (1 OZ) SULTANAS 150 ML (¼ PINT) APPLE OR ORANGE JUICE | 1 SMALL APPLE | 250 G (8 OZ) LOW-FAT NATURAL YOGURT 30 G (GENEROUS 1 OZ) MIXED ALMONDS, HAZELNUTS AND WALNUTS, CHOPPED

1. Put the oats and sultanas in a bowl and add the juice. Cover and leave overnight in the fridge to soak.

2. In the morning, peel the apple and grate it into the oat mixture. You'll find it easier to grate if you don't core or quarter it first, because you'll have something to hang onto. Stir well, then add the yogurt and mix thoroughly. Divide the muesli into 2 serving bowls.

3. Put a dry frying pan over a high heat. When the pan is hot, add the chopped nuts and toast them, stirring so they don't burn. As soon as they begin to smell warm and toasted, scatter them over the muesli. Serve immediately.

B Have a small skimmed milk cappuccino or latte (350 ml/ 12 fl oz) as well and add a drizzle of honey to your muesli (this adds 125 calories)

C Have a small cappuccino or latte and add honey to your muesli, as for B, and have a slice of wholemeal toast with 1 teaspoon low-fat spread as well (this adds 225 calories)

D Have a small cappuccino or latte and add honey to your muesli, as for B, and add 2 slices of toast with low-fat spread, as for C (this adds 325 calories)

Mango & citrus salad

CALORIES PER PORTION   165 kCals

If you like your fruit with a zing, you'll love this yummy sweet-and-sour fruit salad.

SERVES 2   1 orange | 1 GRAPEFRUIT (PINK IF POSSIBLE) | JUICE OF ANOTHER ORANGE | 1 MANGO,

1. Peel the orange and the grapefruit and remove as much of the white pith from the outside as possible. Drop the segments into a mixing bowl, but discard the centres, which can be chewy. Add the orange juice and stir well. Cover the bowl transfer to the fridge for about 1 hour to chill.

2. Peel, stone and chop the mango then add it to the orange and grapefruit; stir gently to combine. Divide the fruit between 2 serving dishes, add any juices from the mixing bowl, and serve immediately.

B Have a slice of wholemeal toast with 1 teaspoon low-fat spread as well (this adds 100 calories)

C Have a boiled egg and a slice of wholemeal toast with 1 teaspoon low-fat spread as well (this adds 190 calories)

D Have a boiled egg and 2 slices of wholemeal toast with low-fat spread as well (this adds 290 calories)

Hot fruit salad with orange juice

CALORIES PER PORTION   280 kCals

Worried about getting your five portions of fruit and veg a day? This will get you off to a flying start. This recipe needs overnight soaking, so start it off the night before.

SERVES 2   100 G (3½ OZ) DRIED APRICOTS (ABOUT 15–20), QUARTERED | 30 G (GENEROUS 1 OZ) SULTANAS
30 G (GENEROUS 1 OZ) RAISINS | 3 DATES, CHOPPED | 300 ML (½ PINT) UNSWEETENED ORANGE JUICE
2 HEAPED TABLESPOONS LOW-FAT GREEK YOGURT

1. Put the apricots, sultanas, raisins and dates in a bowl and add 100 ml (3½ fl oz) of the orange juice; stir well. Cover and leave overnight in the fridge to soak.

2. In the morning, tip the contents of the bowl into a small non-stick saucepan and set it over a medium heat. Add the remaining orange juice and bring to a simmer. Continue to cook gently for 4–5 minutes, and add a little water if necessary to prevent the fruit from catching. Serve immediately, with 1 tablespoon yogurt spooned on the side of each serving.

B Have a slice of wholemeal toast with 1 teaspoon low-fat spread as well (this adds 100 calories)

C Have a slice of wholemeal toast with 1 teaspoon peanut butter, jam or marmalade as well (this adds 125–130 calories)

D Have 2 slices of toast, with 2 teaspoons peanut butter or jam on each (this adds 250–260 calories)

Breakfast fruit glory

CALORIES PER PORTION 300 kCals

If you're a fan of knickerbocker glories, you'll love this fabulous low-calorie, low-fat version, which is simply bursting with vitamins. This is best served in knickerbocker glory glasses, or in glass bowls.

SERVES 2 1 KIWI FRUIT, PEELED AND CHOPPED | 1 SMALL MANGO, PEELED, STONED AND CHOPPED
1 SMALL BANANA, PEELED AND CHOPPED | 2 TABLESPOONS UNSWEETENED ORANGE JUICE
150 G (5 OZ) LOW-FAT GREEK YOGURT | 4 TEASPOONS FLAKED ALMONDS | 2 TEASPOONS CLEAR HONEY

1. Put all of the chopped fruit in a mixing bowl. Gently mix all the fruits together and add the orange juice. Cover and leave in the fridge to chill for 30 minutes.

2. Divide the fruit between 2 knickerbocker glory glasses or small glass bowls, then top each one with half of the yogurt. Scatter the flaked almonds over the yogurt, and then drizzle a teaspoon of honey on top of each. Serve immediately.

B Have a slice of wholemeal toast with 1 teaspoon low-fat spread as well (this adds 100 calories)

C Have a slice of wholemeal toast and 1 teaspoon peanut butter or jam as well (this adds 125–130 calories)

D Have 2 slices of toast with 1 teaspoon peanut butter or jam on each as well (this adds 250–260 calories)

Breakfast bagels

CALORIES PER PORTION with filling 1: 325 Kcals; with filling 2: 310 kCals; with filling 3: 345kCals

Choose from our three tasty fillings for a breakfast you can eat on the run – perfect for days when you have an early start.

SERVES 1

PLAIN BAGEL

FILLING 1: 25 G (1 OZ) SMOKED SALMON | 45 G (3 TABLESPOONS) PLAIN LIGHT CREAM CHEESE
FRESHLY GROUND BLACK PEPPER | A SQUEEZE OF LEMON JUICE, TO TASTE

FILLING 2: 45 G (3 TABLESPOONS) PLAIN LIGHT CREAM CHEESE | 1 RIPE TOMATO, SLICED | A BASIL SPRIG, LEAVES ONLY

FILLING 3: 1 HARD-BOILED EGG, SHELLED AND ROUGHLY CHOPPED | 1 HEAPED TEASPOON LIGHT MAYONNAISE
1 SPRING ONION, FINELY CHOPPED | FRESHLY GROUND BLACK PEPPER

1. Slice the bagel horizontally across; do not add butter or low-fat spread.

2. For Filling 1, spread most of the cream cheese on the bottom half of the bagel, top with the smoked salmon, add some black pepper and then scrape the remaining cream cheese onto the underside of the top half of the bagel. Sandwich together and serve immediately.

3. For Filling 2, fill the bagel with cream cheese as for Filling 1. Top the bottom half with sliced tomato and tear the basil leaves on top. Sandwich together and serve immediately.

4. For Filling 3, put the chopped egg in a bowl with the mayo; mash together with a fork. Add the spring onion and black pepper and mix well. Fill the bagel with the egg mixture and serve immediately.

B Have a small skimmed milk cappuccino or latte (350 ml/ 12 fl oz) as well (this adds 100 calories)

C Have a small cappuccino or latte, as for B, and choose a seeded bagel, if you like them, instead of the plain (this adds 170 calories)

D Have a small cappuccino or latte and choose a seeded bagel, as for B, and also have an apple (this adds 220 calories)

Baked eggs & wholemeal toast

CALORIES PER PORTION 340 kCals

Baked eggs make a nice change from fried, boiled or poached. You'll need some small ovenproof dishes for this recipe.

SERVES 2 2 LARGE EGGS | A LITTLE BUTTER, OR THE WRAPPER FROM A PACK, FOR GREASING | A FEW CHIVES, SNIPPED
SALT AND FRESHLY GROUND BLACK PEPPER   SERVE WITH: 2 SLICES OF WHOLEMEAL TOAST PER PERSON

1. Preheat the oven to 180°C (350°F) Gas mark 4 and boil a kettle of water. Put a sliver of butter on a piece of greaseproof paper (or use a butter wrapper). Grease the insides of 2 small ovenproof dishes or ramekins well, covering every surface. You'll find a little butter goes a long way.

2. Partly fill a small baking tray with boiling water. Crack an egg into each ovenproof dish and put the dishes in the baking tray – the water should

come halfway up the sides. Put the baking tray in the oven and bake for 10–12 minutes. To test if the eggs are ready, tip a dish slightly – the white should just hold.

3. Take the tray out of the oven and remove the dishes. Sprinkle each dish with some chives and add seasoning. Serve immediately, accompanied by toast.

B Have a low-fat natural yogurt as well (this adds 75 calories)

C Have a 300 ml (½ pint) glass of fresh unsweetened orange juice as well (this adds 110 calories)

D Have both the yogurt and the orange juice as in B and C (this adds 185 calories)

Cheese omelette

CALORIES PER PORTION 360 kCals

Cheddar cheese has a nice strong flavour and is easy to grate, but you can substitute your favourite hard cheese, so long as you don't use more than 20 g (¾ oz).

SERVES 1 2 LARGE EGGS | 1 TEASPOON WATER | 20 G (¾ OZ) CHEDDAR CHEESE, GRATED
10 G (⅓ OZ) BUTTER | SALT AND FRESHLY GROUND BLACK PEPPER

1. Beat the eggs in a bowl with the water, a little salt and plenty of black pepper. Add two-thirds of the grated cheese to the egg and beat again.

2. Melt the butter in a small non-stick frying pan. When it begins to froth, pour the eggs into the pan. Swirl them around, then leave them alone for a few seconds. Stir them gently now, drawing the mixture in from the side towards the middle of the pan as the omelette cooks. Tilt the pan

around, letting uncooked liquid run to the edges. Stop stirring when the eggs begin to really set – this won't take long – and cook for about a minute more.

3. Scatter the rest of the cheese on one side of the omelette, fold the other side over it, and lift or slide the omelette gently onto a serving plate. Serve immediately.

B Have a slice of wholemeal toast with 1 teaspoon low-fat spread as well (this adds 100 calories)

C Have 2 slices of wholemeal toast with 1 teaspoon low-fat spread on each as well (this adds 200 calories)

D Add 20 g (¾ oz) Cheddar cheese to the omelette and serve with 2 slices of toast, as in C (this adds 285 calories)

Scrambled eggs & smoked salmon

CALORIES PER PORTION 325 kCals,

The classic luxury breakfast for days when you feel like treating yourself.

SERVES 1 2 SMOKED SALMON SLICES, ABOUT 50 G (2 OZ) | 1 SLIVER OF BUTTER (NOT MORE THAN 10 G/¾ OZ)

2 MEDIUM EGGS | SALT AND FRESHLY GROUND BLACK PEPPER

1. Cut the smoked salmon into strips and set them aside.

2. Melt the butter in a small non-stick saucepan. Crack the eggs into a jug and beat them well, using a fork. When the butter begins to froth, swirl it around the pan and pour the eggs in immediately. Stir the eggs continuously with a wooden spoon, making sure they don't stick anywhere.

3. Remove the pan from the heat before the eggs are completely done, as they will continue to cook in the pan. Season with salt and pepper. Stir the eggs once more, then put them on a plate and scatter with the salmon. Serve immediately.

B Have a slice of wholemeal toast with 1 teaspoon low-fat spread as well (this adds 100 calories)

C Have 2 slices of wholemeal toast with 1 teaspoon low-fat spread on each as well (this adds 200 calories)

D Have 2 slices of toast with low-fat spread, as in C, and add a 300 ml (½ pint) glass of unsweetened orange juice (this adds 310 calories)

Salads & Vegetables

Salsas

Stir these crunchy salsas into green salad to add a little spice as an alternative when a simple oil and vinegar or lemon juice dressing is suggested, or serve them as a dip with crudités. Always remember to add the calories per portion for the salsa to the rest of your meal.

Tomato & onion salsa

CALORIES PER PORTION 90 kCals

SERVES 2 1 TEASPOON LEMON JUICE | 1 TEASPOON BALSAMIC VINEGAR | 2 TEASPOONS OLIVE OIL
1 SMALL RED ONION, FINELY CHOPPED | 2 LARGE RIPE TOMATOES, FINELY CHOPPED
A HANDFUL OF FRESH PARSLEY, FINELY CHOPPED

1. Mix the lemon juice, vinegar and olive oil in a bowl. Add the onion, stir well and leave in the fridge to chill for 30 minutes.

2. Add the tomatoes and the parsley, stir well again, and use within about 10–15 minutes.

Herb salsa

CALORIES PER PORTION 80 kCals

SERVES 2 A BUNCH OF FRESH FLAT-LEAF PARSLEY | SEVERAL BASIL SPRIGS | 1 LARGE SHALLOT, FINELY CHOPPED
1 TEASPOON WHITE WINE VINEGAR | 1 TABLESPOON OLIVE OIL

1. Chop the parsley and basil leaves as finely as possible – be careful if you use a food processor or blender, as it will easily turn to mush.

2. Put the chopped herbs in a bowl and add the shallot. Stir them together and then add the vinegar and olive oil. Mix everything together well, cover the bowl with clingfilm and leave in the fridge for 20 minutes for the flavours to develop. Use within about 10–15 minutes.

Onion & garlic salsa

CALORIES PER PORTION 95 kCals

SERVES 2 20 FAT BLACK OLIVES IN BRINE, PITTED | 1–2 GARLIC CLOVES, FINELY CHOPPED OR CRUSHED
1 TEASPOON MIXED DRIED HERBS | 1 TEASPOON LEMON JUICE | 2 TEASPOONS OLIVE OIL

1. Chop the olives finely – it's best not to use a food processor or blender for this, as it shouldn't end up as a smooth paste.

2. Put the olives in a bowl, add the garlic and dried herbs, and mix. Add the lemon juice and olive oil, and stir everything together.

3. Cover the bowl with clingfilm and leave for 20–30 minutes before using so the flavours can develop.

Salad Dressings

Make these salad dressings in larger quantities and store in the fridge for a few days if you wish, but be careful not to use more than one serving at a time or the calorie count of your dish will rocket! Always remember to add the calories per portion for the dressing to the rest of your meal.

Mustard dressing

CALORIES PER PORTION 70 kCals

SERVES 2 1 TABLESPOON OLIVE OIL | 1 TEASPOON BALSAMIC VINEGAR
1 TEASPOON WHOLEGRAIN MUSTARD, OR TO TASTE

1. Pour the oil and vinegar into a small jar and add the mustard. Put the lid on – make sure it is firmly closed – and shake until the ingredients are combined.

Vinaigrette

CALORIES PER PORTION 70 kCals

SERVES 2 1 TABLESPOON OLIVE OIL | 1 TEASPOON WHITE WINE VINEGAR | ½ TEASPOON FRENCH MUSTARD
A SMALL PINCH OF SUGAR

1. Put the oil, vinegar, mustard and a tiny pinch of sugar in a small jar. Put the lid on – making sure it is firmly closed – and shake until the ingredients are combined and the sugar has dissolved.

Tomato & onion salsa

Vinaigrette

Italian bread & tomato salad

CALORIES PER PORTION 265 kCals

The chunks of bread soak up all the lovely juices, making this a refreshing and satisfying salad.

SERVES 2 2 SLICES OF CRUSTY BREAD, SUCH AS CIABATTA, WEIGHING ABOUT 50 G (2 OZ) EACH
1 GARLIC CLOVE, PEELED (OPTIONAL) | 3 TEASPOONS OLIVE OIL | 3 RIPE TOMATOES, CHOPPED
1 SMALL RED ONION, FINELY CHOPPED | 1 CELERY STICK, CHOPPED | 5 CM (2 INCH) LENGTH OF CUCUMBER, CHOPPED
6 BLACK OLIVES, PITTED AND ROUGHLY CHOPPED | 1 TEASPOON BALSAMIC VINEGAR
SALT AND FRESHLY GROUND BLACK PEPPER

SERVE WITH: COS LETTUCE

1. Preheat the grill to high. Put the slices of bread (slightly stale bread is ideal) under the hot grill for a few seconds on each side to crisp them up a little, but don't allow them to brown.

2. Rub the surface of the bread with the garlic and then cut the bread into small chunks, each one with some of the crust, if possible.

3. Put 1 teaspoon of the olive oil in a large bowl and add the bread – stir it around to coat the bread. Add the chopped vegetables and the olives, the remaining olive oil and the balsamic vinegar, and stir everything together well. Season with some salt and pepper and set the bowl to one side for 10 minutes.

4. Put some cos lettuce on each plate. Spoon the bread salad on top, dividing it between the plates, and serve immediately.

B Use another 50 g (2 oz) slice of ciabatta in the salad (this adds 135 calories)

C Make garlic bread to eat with your salad by toasting half a small ciabatta (about 40 g/1½ oz), rubbing it with a garlic clove and drizzling 1 teaspoon olive oil on top, and add two extra tomatoes to the salad (this adds 190 calories)

D Have garlic bread and extra tomatoes, as for C, and also add another 50 g (2 oz) slice of ciabatta in the salad (this adds 325 calories)

Feta cheese & lentil salad

CALORIES PER PORTION 500 kCals

Lentils fill you up without being heavy in calories, so they make a perfect Biggest Loser lunch. This salad could be taken to work in a lunchbox and served cold.

SERVES 2 1½ TABLESPOONS OLIVE OIL | JUICE OF HALF A LEMON | 1 X 200 G (7 OZ) BLOCK OF FETA CHEESE
100 G (3½ OZ) SMALL GREEN LENTILS (OR PUY LENTILS) | 1 GARLIC CLOVE, HALVED
1 SMALL RED ONION, FINELY CHOPPED | 1 BAY LEAF | A SPRIG OF FRESH MINT
SALT AND FRESHLY GROUND BLACK PEPPER

SERVE WITH: STRONGLY FLAVOURED SALAD LEAVES, SUCH AS BABY SPINACH, WATERCRESS OR ROCKET

1. Put 1 tablespoon of olive oil and the lemon juice in a bowl. Rinse the feta cheese, pat dry, break it up into small chunks and add it to the bowl. Carefully turn the cheese around in the oil and lemon juice, and then cover the bowl and set aside until needed.

2. Pick over the lentils, checking for any grains or small stones. Rinse them under running water and put them in a saucepan of fresh water; add the garlic, red onion and bay leaf. Set aside a few small mint leaves, and add the remaining sprig to the saucepan. Bring to the boil and skim off any froth that forms. Reduce the heat to a simmer and cook the lentils until they are soft; how long

this takes depends on the age of the lentils, but it should not be more than 30 minutes.

3. Drain the cooked lentils and remove the pieces of garlic, the bay leaf and what is left of the mint sprig. Put the lentils in a bowl, add the remaining olive oil and mix together well. Check the seasoning, and carefully stir in the marinated feta and any marinade left in the bowl.

4. Put some salad leaves on each plate, then divide the lentil mixture between them. Top the lentils with the reserved mint leaves and serve immediately while the lentils are still warm.

B Have half a standard wholemeal pitta bread, warmed, as well (this adds 75 calories)

C Have half a wholemeal roll with 1 teaspoon low-fat spread as well (this adds 140 calories). In addition you could also increase the quantity of feta used in the recipe to 300 g (10 oz) for 2 servings (this adds 265 calories)

D Add the same as for C, but have the entire wholemeal roll (this adds 405 calories)

Grilled goats' cheese on a bed of rocket

CALORIES PER PORTION 430 kCals

The creaminess of the goats' cheese, the peppery taste of rocket and the fruitiness of the vinegar make a winning combination.

SERVES 2 1 SLICE FROM A LOG OF GOATS' CHEESE, ABOUT 1.5 CM (¾ INCH) THICK | 1 WHOLEMEAL ROLL
2 TEASPOONS OLIVE OIL | 1 PACK OF ROCKET LEAVES | 4 CHERRY TOMATOES, CHOPPED
1 TEASPOON BALSAMIC VINEGAR | SALT AND FRESHLY GROUND BLACK PEPPER

1. Preheat the grill to high. Carefully slice the goats' cheese in two horizontally – using a clean, wet knife will make this easier. Cut a sliver off the top of the wholemeal roll (so that the top half will stand up as well as the bottom half), and halve the roll horizontally. Put a piece of kitchen foil on the grill and place both halves of roll on it, cut side up. Top each roll with a slice of cheese.

2. Put the olive oil in a little dish and then brush the top of the goats' cheese with some of it. Grill the rolls under the hot grill.

3. Meanwhile, divide the rocket between 2 plates. Scatter the cherry tomatoes over the leaves, drizzle with the balsamic vinegar and whatever oil remains in the little dish. By now the goats' cheese should be browning and bubbling.

4. Remove the grill pan from the heat and carefully put one of the grilled goats' cheese rolls on top of the rocket on the first plate. Repeat with the other, season with salt and plenty of black pepper, and serve immediately.

B Add a little more dressing: use 2 teaspoons olive oil on each roll, and a little more balsamic vinegar (this adds 50 calories)

C Have a thicker slice of goats' cheese, roughly 2 cm (just under 1 inch), divided between the 2 servings (this adds 160 calories)

D Use 2 teaspoons olive oil and a thicker slice of cheese, as for C, divided between the 2 servings (this adds 210 calories)

Greek summer salad

CALORIES PER PORTION 425 kCals

Some people find raw green pepper indigestible, so you can substitute a red or yellow pepper if you wish, or leave it out completely and add an extra tomato.

SERVES 2 4 RIPE TOMATOES, CHOPPED | 1 LARGE GREEN PEPPER, DESEEDED AND CHOPPED (OPTIONAL)
1 ONION, CUT IN HALF AND SLICED | HALF A CUCUMBER, CUT IN HALF LENGTHWAYS AND THINLY SLICED
1 TABLESPOON OLIVE OIL | 1 TEASPOON BALSAMIC VINEGAR | 1 X 200 G (7 OZ) BLOCK OF FETA CHEESE
10 BLACK OLIVES, PITTED AND HALVED | A FEW BASIL LEAVES | FRESHLY GROUND BLACK PEPPER

SERVE WITH: COS LETTUCE OR MIXED LEAVES

1. Put the chopped tomatoes, green pepper, if using, onion and cucumber in a bowl. Put the oil and vinegar in a little jar with a lid, seal the jar – making sure it is firmly closed – and shake it vigorously to make a dressing. Pour the dressing over the vegetables and stir it in gently. Take the feta cheese out of its pack and rinse it under the cold tap, then pat it dry.

2. Put some lettuce leaves on each plate. Divide the dressed vegetables between the 2 plates, then cut the feta in half and crumble half over each salad. Scatter the olives over the salads, and then add a few basil leaves. Check the seasoning – you probably won't need to add salt because of the brine in which the feta is packed – and serve immediately.

B Add half a standard wholemeal pitta bread per serving (this adds 75 calories)

C Add a whole standard wholemeal pitta bread (stuffing it with the salad) per serving (this adds 150 calories)

D Add a whole standard wholemeal pitta bread per serving, increase the quantity of feta cheese to 300 g (10 oz) for 2 servings and add another 2 tomatoes and 6 olives to the salad (this adds 335 calories)

Apple & cabbage slaw with cold chicken

CALORIES PER PORTION for the slaw: 175 kCals; for the chicken 150 kCal

This fruity, tangy coleslaw would work equally well with grilled salmon or some leftover meat from a Sunday roast – don't forget to adjust your total calorie intake.

SERVES 2 1 TABLESPOON OLIVE OIL | 2 CHICKEN BREASTS, WEIGHING ABOUT 125 G (4 OZ) EACH
100 G (3½ OZ) CABBAGE, SHREDDED | 100 G (3½ OZ) CARROT, PEELED | 2 CELERY STICKS, FINELY CHOPPED
4 SPRING ONIONS OR 1 SMALL RED ONION, FINELY CHOPPED | 1 TABLESPOON LOW-FAT GREEK YOGURT
2 TABLESPOONS FULL-FAT MAYONNAISE | 1 LARGE RED DESSERT APPLE | SALT AND FRESHLY GROUND BLACK PEPPER

1. Cook the chicken in advance. Preheat the oven to 200°C (400°F) Gas mark 6. Put the olive oil in an ovenproof dish. Rinse the chicken breasts and pat them dry, then turn them in the oil so they are evenly coated. Put the dish in the preheated oven and roast for 15 minutes. Turn the chicken breasts over and cook the undersides for a further 5 minutes. Check that they are done, which will depend on their size – a knife inserted in the thickest part of the fillet should produce a little clear liquid. Take them out and allow them to cool, then cover and refrigerate until needed.

2. Put the cabbage, carrot, celery and onion in a bowl. Add the yogurt and mayonnaise and stir everything together well. Then grate the apple into the slaw – don't peel or quarter it, just hold it at the top and bottom and grate it. Stir in the grated apple, working quickly so it doesn't begin to discolour. Check the seasoning and add plenty of black pepper.

3. Divide the slaw between 2 plates. Cut each cold chicken breast into slices and arrange them alongside. Serve immediately.

B Have a slice of wholemeal bread with 1 teaspoon low-fat spread as well (this adds 100 calories)

C Have 2 slices of wholemeal bread with 2 teaspoons low-fat spread as well (this adds 200 calories)

D Have a small wholemeal roll with 2 teaspoons low-fat spread as well (this adds 280 calories)

Pear, blue cheese & walnut salad

CALORIES PER PORTION 390 kCals

If you are taking this as a packed lunch, transport the ingredients separately
and assemble just before you want to eat.

SERVES 2 1 TABLESPOON OLIVE OIL | 1 TEASPOON BALSAMIC VINEGAR | A BAG OF STRONGLY FLAVOURED SALAD LEAVES
2 LARGE PEARS, RIPE BUT STILL FIRM | 100 G (3½ OZ) ROQUEFORT CHEESE, OR OTHER BLUE CHEESE
30 G (GENEROUS 1 OZ) WALNUTS, CHOPPED | SALT AND FRESHLY GROUND BLACK PEPPER

1. Put the oil and vinegar in a small jar, twist the lid on – making sure it is firmly closed – and shake it vigorously.

2. Wash and drain the salad leaves and spread them on the 2 serving plates. Cut the pears into quarters, remove the cores and chop them into pieces; scatter these over the salad leaves.

3. Cut the cheese in two and crumble half evenly over each plate. Scatter half the walnuts over each salad.

4. Finally give the jar of dressing another shake and drizzle it over the salads. Add a little salt and a good grinding of black pepper, and serve immediately.

B Add another 10 g (½ oz) walnuts per serving (this adds 55 calories)

C Have a slice of granary bread with 1 teaspoon low-fat spread as well, and the extra walnuts, as for B (this adds 155 calories)

D Keep the same walnut quantities as the recipe but have an entire wholemeal roll with 2 teaspoons low-fat spread with the salad (this adds 280 calories)

Warm chickpea, beetroot & onion salad

CALORIES PER PORTION 275 kCals

This substantial salad is both filling and tasty. Try to find baby beetroot that are no bigger than golf balls.

SERVES 2 · 200 G (7 OZ) RAW BEETROOT, AS SMALL AS POSSIBLE
1 X 400 G (13 OZ) CAN OF CHICKPEAS, DRAINED AND RINSED | 1 RED ONION, SLICED | SALAD LEAVES
SALT AND FRESHLY GROUND BLACK PEPPER

FOR THE DRESSING: 2 TEASPOONS OLIVE OIL | A DRIZZLE OF BALSAMIC VINEGAR

1. Preheat the oven to 180°C (350°F) Gas mark 4.

2. Clean the beetroot carefully, trying not to break the skin, and trim the leaves. Wrap each one in foil, place the little parcels in an ovenproof dish and put in the preheated oven for 1 hour, or until they are soft.

3. Remove the beetroot from the oven and put them aside, still wrapped, until they are cool enough to handle. Unwrap them when they are ready, trim the tops and bottoms of the beetroot and slide off their skins. Set the beets aside.

4. Put the chickpeas in a saucepan, cover them with fresh water and warm them through over a medium heat for 3–4 minutes. If you don't like raw onion, add the onion to the pan to cook, too. Drain the chickpeas and put them in a bowl, then add the dressing ingredients and stir well.

5. Put some salad leaves on each plate. Chop the warm beetroot and scatter most of it over the salad. Then scatter the onions over the salad and spoon the chickpeas on top. Drizzle any dressing left in the bowl over the salad. Put the remaining beets on top, and season with salt and pepper.

B Have a slice of toasted wholemeal bread with the salad, or cut it into croutons and scatter them over the salad leaves with the onions and beets (this adds 100 calories)

C Have half a wholemeal roll with 1 teaspoon low-fat spread (this adds 140 calories)

D Have a whole wholemeal roll with 2 teaspoons low-fat spread (this adds 280 calories)

Couscous salad

CALORIES PER PORTION 300 kCals

The flavours mingle beautifully in this easy-to-prepare salad. It's good served at a barbecue or as part of a buffet when you're entertaining.

SERVES 2 100 G (3½ OZ) COUSCOUS | 125 ML (4 FL OZ) HOT WATER | 1 TEASPOON TOMATO PURÉE
JUICE OF HALF A LEMON | 1 TABLESPOON OLIVE OIL | 3 RIPE TOMATOES, FINELY CHOPPED
HALF A CUCUMBER, FINELY CHOPPED | 1 RED ONION, FINELY CHOPPED
1 RED CHILLI, DESEEDED AND VERY FINELY CHOPPED (OPTIONAL)
A LARGE HANDFUL OF FLAT-LEAF PARSLEY, CHOPPED | A SPRIG OF MINT, LEAVES ONLY, CHOPPED
SALT AND FRESHLY GROUND BLACK PEPPER

SERVE WITH: COS LETTUCE

1. Put the couscous in a large bowl and add the hot water and tomato purée. Stir well, cover with clingfilm and set aside for 5 minutes. By the end of this time the couscous should have absorbed all the water, but if it has not, drain it with a sieve. Put the couscous back in the bowl and fluff it up with a fork to break up any lumps. Add the lemon juice and oil and stir well. Cover with clingfilm and set aside for the couscous to cool and the flavours to blend.

2. Put all of the vegetables in a bowl, then add the chopped parsley and mint.

3. Just before serving, add the vegetables and herbs to the couscous and mix together. Check for seasoning and add salt and pepper to taste. Serve on a bed of cos lettuce.

Note: Wash your hands immediately after chopping the chilli; be very careful not to touch your eyes or any other sensitive place before doing so, as chilli juices can sting.

B Increase the total amount of couscous to 150 g (5 oz) and have half a standard wholemeal pitta bread per serving as well (this adds 165 calories)

C Increase the total amount of couscous, as for B, and have a whole standard wholemeal pitta bread (stuffing it with the salad) per serving as well (this adds 240 calories)

D Increase the total amount of couscous to 200 g (7 oz), have a whole standard wholemeal pitta bread per serving as well, and add 2 extra tomatoes to the recipe (this adds 350 calories)

Rocket, tomato, borlotti bean & chicken salad

CALORIES PER PORTION 350 kCals

If you are taking this as a packed lunch, carry the rocket and salad leaves separately and make up the salad when you are ready to eat.

SERVES 2 1 TEASPOON OLIVE OIL | 2 CHICKEN BREASTS, ABOUT 100 G (3½ OZ) EACH | JUICE OF 1 LEMON
1 X 400 G (13 OZ) CAN OF BORLOTTI BEANS, DRAINED AND RINSED | 3 TEASPOONS OLIVE OIL
2 TEASPOONS BALSAMIC VINEGAR | 1 GARLIC CLOVE, CUT IN HALF | 1 X SMALL BAG OF ROCKET
1 X BAG OF MIXED SALAD LEAVES | 4 RIPE TOMATOES, CHOPPED | 1 SMALL RED ONION, CHOPPED
SALT AND FRESHLY GROUND BLACK PEPPER

1. Cook the chicken in advance. Preheat the oven to 200°C (400°F) Gas mark 6. Put the oil in an ovenproof dish, rinse the chicken breasts and pat them dry. Put most of the lemon juice in the dish as well, then turn the chicken breasts in the oil and lemon mixture so they are evenly coated. Pour over the rest of the juice.

2. Put the dish in the preheated oven and roast for 15 minutes, then turn the chicken breasts over and cook the undersides for a further 5 minutes. Turn them over once more and allow the tops to colour a little. Check that the chicken breasts are done, which will depend on their size – a knife inserted in the thickest part of the fillet should produce a little clear liquid. Take them out and leave them to cool, then cover and refrigerate until needed.

3. Put the beans in a saucepan of water, bring to a simmer and cook for a couple of minutes. Drain them and put them in a bowl. Add 1 teaspoon each of the olive oil and balsamic vinegar, and stir everything together. Set the beans aside to cool.

4. Rub the inside of a large bowl with the cut surfaces of the garlic (discard the garlic after this). Put the rocket and the mixed leaves in the bowl, then add the tomatoes and red onion. Add the rest of the olive oil and balsamic vinegar, and mix everything together. Now add the borlotti beans, and mix them in as well.

5. Cut the chicken breasts into chunks and add them to the bowl. Add a little salt and black pepper. Mix everything together once more, thoroughly but quite gently, and serve immediately.

B Have half a small ciabatta, about 40 g (1½ oz) as well (this adds 110 calories)

C Have half a small wholemeal roll with 1 teaspoon low-fat spread as well (this adds 140 calories)

D Have an entire small wholemeal roll with 2 teaspoons low-fat spread as well (this adds 280 calories)

Black-eyed bean salad with red onion & hard-boiled egg

CALORIES PER PORTION 440 kCals

Use canned beans if you prefer – about one-and-a-half tins, well rinsed and drained. Simmer them in a little water for 5–10 minutes with the onion and bay leaf.

SERVES 2 125 G (4 OZ) DRIED BLACK-EYED BEANS | 1 ONION, CHOPPED | 1 BAY LEAF | 2 EGGS
5 TEASPOONS OLIVE OIL | JUICE OF HALF A LEMON | A LARGE HANDFUL OF FLAT-LEAF PARSLEY, CHOPPED
SALT AND FRESHLY GROUND BLACK PEPPER | 10 BLACK OLIVES, PITTED AND HALVED

SERVE WITH: MIXED SALAD LEAVES

1. Soak the beans in plenty of cold water overnight. The next day, drain them and put them in a saucepan, cover with fresh water and bring to the boil. Boil for 10 minutes, removing any scum that forms, and then add the chopped onion and the bay leaf. Lower the heat and simmer for 45–60 minutes, or until the beans are soft. Meanwhile, hard-boil the eggs.

2. Drain the beans and allow them to cool until they are no longer hot but are warm right through. Remove the bay leaf. Put 3 teaspoons of oil, the lemon juice and the chopped parsley in a bowl and mix them well. Then add the drained beans and stir everything together. Cover the beans and leave them to absorb the flavours for 30 minutes.

3. Put some salad leaves on each plate. Check the seasoning of the beans and add salt and black pepper to taste. Stir the beans and then divide them between the 2 plates. Peel the hard-boiled eggs and cut them into quarters. Decorate the salad with the eggs, and then top with the olives. Finally, drizzle a teaspoon of olive oil over each salad and serve immediately.

B Add some extra dressing: add 1 more tablespoon of olive oil and a little more lemon juice, to taste (this adds 120 calories)

C Add some extra dressing, as for B, and have a 50 g (2 oz) slice of ciabatta to soak up the juices as well (this adds 255 calories)

D Add some extra dressing, as for B, and have a whole small ciabatta (no spread necessary), usually about 85 g (3¼ oz) (this adds 350 calories)

Penne with peas, cream & Parmesan

CALORIES PER PORTION 535 kCals,

If you're a fan of macaroni cheese, you'll love this sophisticated version, which is rich and scrumptious.

SERVES 2 200 G (7 OZ) PENNE OR SIMILAR PASTA | 150 G (5 OZ) FROZEN PEAS | 75 ML (3 FL OZ) SINGLE CREAM
25 G (1 OZ) PARMESAN CHEESE, GRATED | SALT AND FRESHLY GROUND BLACK PEPPER

SERVE WITH: SALAD LEAVES

1. Put a large saucepan of water over a medium to high heat, and when it begins to boil add the pasta and a pinch of salt.

2. Meanwhile, put the frozen peas in a sieve and run them under the cold tap to dislodge any excess ice. After the pasta has been cooking for about 5 minutes, put the peas in a separate saucepan, cover with water and bring to the boil. Lower the heat and simmer until they are cooked, about 2–3 minutes.

3. Drain the peas well, return them to the pan and add the cream; warm the cream through but do not allow it to boil. Take the pan off the heat and add half the Parmesan and stir in; the warmth should melt the cheese.

4. Drain the pasta and return it to its pan, then pour the pea, cream and cheese mixture into the pasta and stir everything together well. Check for seasoning and scatter the remaining Parmesan over the pasta. Serve immediately, accompanied by a plain green salad.

B Add a dressing (2 teaspoons olive oil and 1 teaspoon lemon juice) to the green salad (this adds 90 calories)

C Add a salad dressing, as for B, and have half a small wholemeal roll (no spread) to mop up the sauce as well (this adds 230 calories)

D Add a dressing, as for B, have a wholemeal roll, as for C, and use 250 g (8 oz) pasta between 2 servings (this adds 320 calories)

Pasta salad with tuna & peppers

CALORIES PER PORTION 480 kCals

It's fine to prepare this in advance, but don't add the mayonnaise and balsamic vinegar until you are ready to eat.

SERVES 2 150 G (5 OZ) PENNE | A PINCH OF SALT | 1 TEASPOON OLIVE OIL
1 X 185 G (6½ OZ) CAN OF TUNA IN SPRING WATER | 12 BLACK OLIVES, PITTED AND CHOPPED
1 RED PEPPER, DESEEDED AND DICED | 2 TOMATOES, DESEEDED AND CHOPPED
A HANDFUL OF FLAT-LEAF PARSLEY, LEAVES ONLY, FINELY CHOPPED | 3 TABLESPOONS LIGHT MAYONNAISE
1 TEASPOON BALSAMIC VINEGAR | FRESHLY GROUND BLACK PEPPER

SERVE WITH: SALAD LEAVES

1. Put a saucepan of water over a medium to high heat and, when it begins to boil, add the pasta and a pinch of salt. Cook the pasta until it is just ready and still has a slight bite, then drain and rinse under a cold tap. Put it in a large bowl and add the olive oil; stir them together.

2. Drain the tuna and flake it into the bowl with the pasta. Add the olives, pepper, tomatoes and parsley and stir everything together gently with a wooden spoon.

3. In a separate bowl, mix the mayonnaise, balsamic vinegar and plenty of black pepper. Add this mixture to the pasta and stir it in thoroughly with the wooden spoon; serve immediately, accompanied by some salad leaves.

B Have half a small ciabatta, about 40 g (1½ oz), as well (this adds 110 calories)

C Have a whole small ciabatta, about 85 g (3¼ oz), as well (this adds 220 calories)

D Make the salad with 200 g (7 oz) pasta and have a whole small ciabatta, as for C, as well (this adds 310 calories)

Warm potato salad with smoked fish

CALORIES PER PORTION 445 kCals

This is a hearty, flavoursome meal, which could be served cold
as a packed lunch if need be.

SERVES 2 500 G (1 LB) NEW POTATOES | 1 TABLESPOON OLIVE OIL
1 TEASPOON CIDER VINEGAR OR WHITE WINE VINEGAR | 150 G (5 OZ) SMOKED SALMON
3 TABLESPOONS LIGHT MAYONNAISE | ½ –1 TEASPOON FRENCH MUSTARD, OR TO TASTE (OPTIONAL)
6 SPRING ONIONS, CHOPPED | A HANDFUL OF FLAT-LEAF PARSLEY, CHOPPED
SALT AND FRESHLY GROUND BLACK PEPPER

SERVE WITH: MIXED SALAD LEAVES

1. Put a large saucepan of water over a high heat and add a pinch of salt. Cut the bigger potatoes into chunks no larger than 2 cm (just under 1 inch) and add them to the pan. Bring the water to the boil and cook the potatoes until they are just tender, about 10 minutes.

2. Put the oil and vinegar in a small jar with a lid, seal the jar – making sure it is firmly closed – and shake it vigorously to combine.

3. Drain the potatoes well and put them in a large bowl. Pour the dressing over them, stir well and set the bowl to one side for 5 minutes.

4. Cut the smoked salmon into strips and put them in another bowl. Add the mayonnaise, mustard, spring onions and parsley and stir them together gently. Then add this mixture to the potatoes and combine everything carefully, using a wooden spoon. Check the seasoning and add salt and black pepper if necessary.

5. Divide the salad leaves between 2 plates and spoon the warm potato salad on top. Serve immediately.

B Increase the amount of smoked salmon to 200 g (7 oz) and have a slice of wholemeal or granary bread (no spread) as well (this adds 140 calories)

C Increase the amount of smoked salmon, as for B, but use 700 g (1⅓ lb) potatoes in the recipe and add another tablespoon mayonnaise as well (this adds 250 calories)

D Increase the amounts of salmon and potato, as for C, but accompany with a slice of wholemeal bread with 1 teaspoon low-fat spread as well (this adds 350 calories)

Baked potatoes three ways

CALORIES PER PORTION for filling 1: 375 kCals; for filling 2: 405 kCals; for filling 3: 368 kCals

Choose between the three fillings. You can also cook baked potatoes in a microwave but the results are often not as good; follow manufacturers' instructions, and omit the oil.

SERVES 1 **1 POTATO, WEIGHING ABOUT 200 G (7 OZ)** | **A LITTLE OLIVE OIL, NOT MORE THAN 1 TEASPOON**
SALT AND FRESHLY GROUND BLACK PEPPER

FILLING 1: BEANS AND BACON **1 STREAKY BACON RASHER** | **1 X 150 G (5 OZ) CAN OF BAKED BEANS**

FILLING 2: PLOUGHMAN'S POTATO **25 G (1 OZ) STRONG CHEDDAR CHEESE, GRATED**
1 SMALL RED ONION OR 2 SPRING ONIONS, CHOPPED | **1 TABLESPOON CHUTNEY**
1 SLIVER OF BUTTER, NOT MORE THAN 10 G (½ OZ)

FILLING 3: LUXURY LUNCH **50 G (2 OZ) LIGHT CREAM CHEESE** | **1 TABLESPOON LOW-FAT CRÈME FRAÎCHE**
50 G (2 OZ) SMOKED SALMON

1. Preheat the oven to 200°C (400°F) Gas mark 6. Wash and dry the potato. Score a line around it, pierce it in a few places with the knife and then wipe it with a piece of kitchen paper moistened with the olive oil. Put the potato in the oven for 50–60 minutes, or until you can tell it is cooked because it gives when you stick a knife in. Keep warm while you prepare the filling of your choice.

2. To make filling 1, place a frying pan over a high heat, and dry-fry the bacon rasher (no oil), and heat the beans in a small non-stick saucepan. Turn the bacon until it is well done, then hold it above the pan to let the excess fat drain off. Blot it on kitchen paper. Split the potato and spoon the beans on top. Crumble the bacon over the beans, season and serve immediately.

3. To make filling 2, put the grated cheese and onions in a bowl and stir together. Add the chutney and mix it in. Split the potato, add the sliver of butter and fill it with the cheese mixture. Serve immediately.

4. To make filling 3, put the cream cheese and crème fraiche in a bowl and mix them together well. Cut the smoked salmon into pieces, stir them into the mixture and add black pepper to taste. Split the potato and add the filling. Serve immediately.

B Add a green salad with a dressing made from 2 teaspoons olive oil and 1 teaspoon balsamic vinegar (this adds 120 calories)

C Add a salad, as for B, but have a larger potato, about 300–350 g (10–11 ½ oz) as well (this adds 235 calories)

D Have a salad and a larger potato, as for C, and also increase the filling quantities.
Filling 1: have 2 bacon rashers (this adds 305 calories)
Filling 2: have 35 g (1 ½ oz) cheese and heap the tablespoon of chutney (this adds 330 calories)
Filling 3: add another 2 tablespoons low-fat crème fraîche (this adds 290 calories)

Vegetable couscous with tomato & chilli sauce

CALORIES PER PORTION 375 kCals

Harissa paste, made from chillies, is a useful thing to keep in your fridge. At only 7 calories per teaspoon you can afford to add it to any dish when you want a bit of spicy heat.

SERVES 2 | 5 TEASPOONS OLIVE OIL | 1 AUBERGINE, SLICED AND QUARTERED | 1 COURGETTE, CHOPPED
1 RED PEPPER, DESEEDED AND CHOPPED INTO LARGE PIECES | 1 RED ONION, PEELED AND SLICED INTO SECTIONS
1 SHALLOT OR SMALL ONION, CHOPPED | 1 GARLIC CLOVE, FINELY CHOPPED
A PINCH OF CHILLI POWDER, TO TASTE, OR ½ TEASPOON HARISSA PASTE
1 X 227 G (7½ OZ) CAN OF CHOPPED TOMATOES | 100 G (3½ OZ) COUSCOUS | 100 ML (3½ FL OZ) BOILING WATER

SERVE WITH: SALAD LEAVES

1. Preheat the oven to 200°C (400°F) Gas mark 6. Put 2 teaspoons of the olive oil in a large roasting tin or ovenproof dish and pop it in the preheated oven for a minute or two. Take it out, and tilt it so that the olive oil runs across the dish. Put the aubergine, courgette, pepper and onion in the roasting tin and stir them around; drizzle another 2 teaspoons of the oil over them. Return the tin to the oven and cook until the vegetables are just tender – how long this takes will depend on how large the vegetable pieces are, but it should be approximately 40–50 minutes.

2. While the vegetables are cooking, prepare the sauce. Put the remaining olive oil in a small non-stick pan and cook the shallot until it is transparent, about 5 minutes. Then add the garlic and the chilli powder or harissa and mix it in, stirring, for about a minute. Add the tomatoes and simmer gently for 10 more minutes.

3. Push the sauce through a sieve into a small bowl or jug; if necessary, adjust the thickness by adding a little hot water. Discard the pulp remaining in the sieve.

4. When the vegetables are almost ready, prepare the couscous. Put it in a large bowl and add the boiling water. Stir well, cover with clingfilm and set aside for 5 minutes. By the end of this time the couscous should be soft – if it isn't, then leave it a little longer. It should also have absorbed all the water, but if it hasn't, drain it with a sieve. Put the couscous back in the bowl and fluff it up with a fork, breaking up any lumps. Reheat the sauce if necessary, but don't let it burn.

5. Divide the couscous between 2 plates, and put the roasted vegetables on top. Pour the sauce over everything and serve immediately accompanied by a green salad.

B Add a dressing to the salad (2 teaspoons olive oil and 1 teaspoon lemon juice) as well (this adds 90 calories)

C Add a dressing, as for B, and increase the amount of couscous to 140 g (4¾ oz) as well (this adds 160 calories)

D Add a dressing and increase the amount of couscous, as for C, but also roast 2 chicken breasts, about 100 g (3½ oz) in the oven (see page 58) at the same time as the vegetables (this adds 310 calories)

Spinach, smoky bacon & poached egg salad

CALORIES PER PORTION 355 kCals

If you want to cook your egg in an egg poacher, you'll have to coat it with a light spray of oil so the egg doesn't stick.

SERVES 1 2 HANDFULS OF BABY SPINACH LEAVES, ANY STRINGY STALKS REMOVED
2 SMOKED STREAKY BACON RASHERS | 1 EGG

FOR THE DRESSING: 2 TEASPOONS OLIVE OIL | A DRIZZLE OF CIDER VINEGAR
A PINCH OF WHOLEGRAIN MUSTARD | FRESHLY GROUND BLACK PEPPER

1. Whisk the dressing ingredients together in a small bowl or jug and add a little black pepper to taste.

2. Wash the spinach leaves, shake them dry and put them on a serving plate.

3. Place a frying pan over a high heat, and dry-fry the bacon (no oil) until it is well done. Remove from the pan, then hold it above the pan to let the excess fat drain off. Blot it on kitchen paper and set aside.

3. Fill a saucepan with about 4 cm (2 inches) of water and put it over a medium heat, then crack the egg into a small bowl. When the water is simmering, slide the egg into the middle (swirling the water first to help keep the white together). Cook until the egg white is set – about 2 minutes.

4. While the egg is poaching, crumble the bacon over the spinach leaves and drizzle the dressing on top. When the egg is ready, remove it from the water using a slotted spoon and put it briefly on some kitchen paper to drain. Lay it on the salad and serve immediately.

B Toast a slice of sourdough bread or ciabatta (about 40 g/1 ½ oz), rub it with garlic and cut into small croutons, then sprinkle over the salad as well (this adds 100–125 calories).

C Add croutons, as for B, plus add an extra handful of spinach leaves and one more streaky bacon rasher (this adds 175–200 calories).

D Add croutons and more bacon and spinach, as for C, but have 2 slices of sourdough or ciabatta bread (this adds 275–325 calories)

Paprika mushrooms on toast with a great big salad

CALORIES PER PORTION just for the mushrooms: 335 kCals; just for the salad: 150 kCals (125 kCals without the olives)

You haven't lived until you've tasted this dish! It's truly delicious. Trust us!

SERVES 1 **2 SMALL INDIVIDUAL CIABATTAS, ABOUT 75 G (3 OZ) EACH** | **2 TEASPOONS OLIVE OIL**
1 ONION, FINELY CHOPPED | **2 GARLIC CLOVES, FINELY CHOPPED** | **500 G (1 LB) BUTTON MUSHROOMS, SLICED**
A SPRIG OF FRESH THYME | **½ TEASPOON PAPRIKA, OR MORE TO TASTE** | **A SQUEEZE OF LEMON JUICE**
2 TABLESPOONS LOW-FAT CRÈME FRAÎCHE | **SALT AND FRESHLY GROUND BLACK PEPPER**

FOR THE SALAD: **1 LARGE BAG OF STRONGLY FLAVOURED SALAD LEAVES** | **3 LARGE RIPE TOMATOES, QUARTERED**
1 RED PEPPER, DESEEDED AND FINELY SLICED | **HALF A CUCUMBER, SLICED**
10 BLACK OLIVES, PITTED AND HALVED (OPTIONAL) | **6 SPRING ONIONS, CHOPPED (OPTIONAL)**
1 TABLESPOON OLIVE OIL | **1 TEASPOON LEMON JUICE** | **SALT AND FRESHLY GROUND BLACK PEPPER**

1. Make up the salad first, as the mushrooms are quick to cook. Wash and dry the leaves and put them in a large bowl. Add the tomatoes, pepper slices, cucumber, olives and spring onions, if using. Put the oil and lemon juice in a small jar with a pinch of salt and some black pepper, seal – making sure it is firmly closed – then shake until the oil and lemon are combined. Pour over the salad and mix everything together. Cover and set aside.

2. Cut the two ciabattas in half horizontally and and preheat the grill to high. Heat the oil in a large non-stick frying pan and gently fry the onion for 5 minutes, then add the garlic. As soon as the garlic begins to take on colour, add the mushrooms to the pan. Remove the leaves from the sprig of thyme and add them too. Cook gently, until the mushroom juices begin to run, then add the paprika and a little lemon juice, plus some salt and black pepper.

3. Put the ciabattas under the hot grill to warm though and slightly toast the cut surfaces.

4. Increase the heat under the frying pan and fry the mushrooms until the liquid has almost all gone and they are beginning to crisp up. Turn off the heat and add the crème fraiche, stirring it in well. Put two pieces of ciabatta on each plate and top with the creamy mushrooms. Serve the salad on the side.

B Use another 2 tablespoons of crème fraîche and cook the mushrooms gently for a couple of minutes more over a very low heat, concentrating the creamy liquid (this adds 25 calories)

C Add more crème fraîche, as for B, and dry-fry a bacon rasher to crumble on top as well (this adds 75 calories)

D Add more crème fraîche, as for B, and dry-fry 2 bacon rashers to crumble on top and add another 250 g (8 oz) mushrooms as well (this adds 160 calories)

Spring vegetable risotto

CALORIES PER PORTION 425 kCals

Risotto is easy to make – you just keep stirring, then adding more liquid, then stirring again until it's ready.

SERVES 2 1 TEASPOON OLIVE OIL | 1 SLIVER OF BUTTER, NOT MORE THAN 10 G (½ OZ)
1 SMALL WHITE ONION OR 2 SHALLOTS | 1 GARLIC CLOVE, VERY FINELY CHOPPED
175 G (6 OZ) RISOTTO RICE (ARBORIO) | 350–400 ML (10–14 FL OZ) BOILING WATER OR HOT VEGETABLE STOCK
50 G (2 OZ) PEAS (DEFROSTED, IF FROZEN) | 50 G (2 OZ) BABY BROAD BEANS (DEFROSTED, IF FROZEN)
2 SMALL COURGETTES, FINELY SLICED | SALT AND FRESHLY GROUND BLACK PEPPER

SERVE WITH: A MIXED GREEN SALAD

1. Put the oil and butter in a large frying pan, and melt over a medium heat. When the butter begins to bubble a little, add the onion and garlic, and cook them very gently for 5 minutes until the onion is just transparent. Add the risotto rice and stir it around so that it is evenly coated.

2. Add about 100 ml (3½ fl oz) of the boiling water or hot stock, and let it bubble for a couple of minutes, stirring. Add the peas and broad beans, then add a little more liquid as soon as the first has been absorbed. Continue cooking the risotto, stirring regularly and adding more liquid every time it looks like drying out, until there is only about 100 ml (3½ fl oz) liquid left. Then add the courgettes and carry on.

3. When almost all the liquid has been absorbed and all the vegetables are tender, take the pan off the heat. Add some salt and pepper to taste, stir it thoroughly, and then serve immediately. Accompany with a green salad.

B Add a dressing to the salad (2 teaspoons olive oil and a drizzle of balsamic vinegar) as well (this adds 90 calories)

C Make the risotto with 200 g (7 oz) arborio rice, plus add a salad dressing as for B, and sprinkle 10 g (½ oz) grated Parmesan over the risotto (this ads 175 calories)

D As for C, but use 225 g 7 ½ oz) risotto rice (this adds 220 calories)

Soups & Stews

Tomato & coriander soup with yogurt

CALORIES PER PORTION 110 kCals (with 2 tablespoons yogurt, 140 kCals)

Swirl in some yogurt if you wish, but remember that all spoon measurements are level rather than heaped.

SERVES 4 1 TABLESPOON OLIVE OIL | 10 SPRING ONIONS (OR ONE BUNCH, IF LARGE), CHOPPED
1 POTATO, ABOUT 100 G (3½ OZ), PEELED AND CHOPPED | 1 GARLIC CLOVE, CRUSHED
A GOOD HANDFUL OF CORIANDER, LEAVES ONLY, FINELY CHOPPED | 1 KG (2 LB) RIPE TOMATOES, CHOPPED
ABOUT 750 ML (1¼ PINTS) WATER | SALT AND FRESHLY GROUND BLACK PEPPER
8 TABLESPOONS LOW-FAT NATURAL YOGURT, TO GARNISH (OPTIONAL)

1. Put the olive oil in a large saucepan over a medium heat and warm it through. Add the spring onions and cook them for 5 minutes, stirring so that they do not catch. Add the potato and the garlic, stir them around and let them cook for a minute or so, and then add the coriander leaves and the tomatoes.

2. Stir everything together for another minute or so, and then add the water. Bring the soup to the boil and simmer for 20 minutes or so, until all the ingredients are very soft.

3. Put a sieve over a clean pan and ladle the soup into it, pressing it through the sieve with the back of the ladle or a wooden spoon.

4. When all the soup has been passed though the sieve, scrape anything remaining on the underside into the pan and discard the remains of the vegetables left in the sieve.

5. Put the pan over a gentle heat, and reheat the soup. Adjust the thickness, if necessary, by adding a little water, and season with salt and pepper. Serve, garnished with a swirl of low-fat natural yogurt, if using.

Carrot & red pepper soup

CALORIES PER PORTION k135 kCals

The sweet flavours of carrots and peppers combine to make an elegant and attractive soup.

SERVES 4 2 TEASPOONS OLIVE OIL | 1 ONION, CHOPPED | 1 GARLIC CLOVE, FINELY CHOPPED
800 G (1 LB 10 OZ) CARROTS, CHOPPED | 2 RED PEPPERS, DESEEDED AND CHOPPED
1 POTATO, CHOPPED | SALT AND FRESHLY GROUND BLACK PEPPER

1. Heat the oil in a heavy-based saucepan over a medium heat. Add the onion and fry until softened, about 5 minutes, stirring to make sure it doesn't catch. Add the garlic after the first couple of minutes.

2. Add the carrots, peppers, potato and enough water to cover the vegetables. Simmer for about 20 minutes until the vegetables are soft.

3. Leave the soup to cool slightly, then transfer to a food processor or blender and whizz until smooth. Check for seasoning, add salt and pepper to taste, reheat and serve.

Butternut squash soup

CALORIES PER PORTION 100 kCals

Butternut squash used to appear in the 'exotic' section of the vegetable aisle in the supermarket, but they are becoming more common as people discover how yummy they are!

SERVES 4 HALF A BUTTERNUT SQUASH, WEIGHING ABOUT 300–400 G (10–13 OZ) | 2 TEASPOONS OLIVE OIL
1 LARGE ONION, CHOPPED | 1 GARLIC CLOVE, FINELY CHOPPED | A PINCH OF PAPRIKA | SALT

8 TABLESPOONS NATURAL YOGURT, TO GARNISH

1. Prepare the squash first. Cut it into sections, pull away the seeds and cut off the skin. Chop any large pieces into smaller chunks.

2. Heat the oil in a large saucepan, add the onion and garlic and cook gently for 5 minutes; don't allow them to burn. Add the pieces of squash to the pan and stir well, then add a pinch of paprika. Stir again and add enough water to cover.

3. Cook for about 20 minutes until the vegetables are soft. Leave the soup to cool slightly, then transfer to a food processor or blender and whizz until smooth. You can adjust the thickness of the soup by adding a little more liquid if necessary. Check for seasoning, adding salt if necessary. Reheat gently and serve, swirling with natural yogurt just beforehand.

Sweet potato & sweetcorn soup

CALORIES PER PORTION 190 kCals

The sweet and earthy flavours work well with a little chilli heat, if you like it. This soup is a good winter warmer that could be taken to work in a flask.

SERVES 3 2 TEASPOONS OLIVE OIL | 1 ONION, FINELY CHOPPED | 1 GARLIC CLOVE, FINELY CHOPPED
HALF A SMALL RED CHILLI, DESEEDED AND VERY FINELY CHOPPED (OPTIONAL)
1 MEDIUM SWEET POTATO, WEIGHING ABOUT 250 G (8 OZ), PEELED AND CHOPPED INTO 1.5 CM (¾ INCH) CHUNKS
700 ML (24 FL OZ) VEGETABLE STOCK OR WATER | 1 X 340 G (11½ OZ) CAN OF SWEETCORN, DRAINED AND RINSED
SALT AND FRESHLY GROUND BLACK PEPPER

1. Heat the oil in a large saucepan over a medium heat. Add the onion and fry for about 5 minutes, or until it has softened, stirring so that it doesn't stick. Add the garlic and the chilli, if using, and cook for another minute or so, stirring.

2. Add the sweet potato, stirring the pieces around in the onion mixture. Add enough water or stock to cover the vegetables, about 400 ml (14 fl oz). Simmer the soup for 10 minutes.

3. Add the sweetcorn and the remaining stock or water. Cook the soup for a further 5 minutes, making sure that all the vegetables are soft. Remove a few sweetcorn kernels for use as a garnish.

4. Add a little salt and pepper to taste, then transfer to a food processor or blender and whizz until smooth. Serve, decorating with the reserved sweetcorn kernels.

Creamy mushroom soup

CALORIES PER PORTION 110 kCals

Choose your favourite type of mushroom – large Portobello mushrooms have a much stronger flavour than small button mushrooms, and chestnut mushrooms have a firmer texture.

SERVES 4 400 G (13 OZ) MUSHROOMS | A SLIVER OF BUTTER, NO MORE THAN 10 G (½ OZ)
1 TEASPOON SUNFLOWER OIL | 1 ONION, CHOPPED | 200 ML (7 FL OZ) VEGETABLE STOCK OR WATER
250 ML (8 FL OZ) SEMI-SKIMMED MILK | 1 THYME SPRIG
SALT AND FRESHLY GROUND BLACK PEPPER | 4 TABLESPOONS SINGLE CREAM, TO GARNISH

1. Trim the ends off the mushroom stalks, clean off any earth and chop the whole mushrooms – stalks and all.

2. Put the butter and oil in a large heavy-based saucepan over a medium heat. When the butter has melted and started to bubble, add the onion. Cook it gently, stirring, for about 5–10 minutes, until softened but not brown.

3. Stir in the mushrooms, and cook for a further 2–3 minutes. Add the stock and milk. Strip the leaves off the thyme sprig and add to the soup.

4. Increase the temperature and bring the soup to the boil, then lower the heat and simmer for about 20 minutes until all the vegetables are soft. Check for seasoning, and add salt and pepper to taste.

5. Leave the soup to cool slightly, then transfer to a food processor or blender and whizz it roughly – it shouldn't be too smooth. Add more water if the soup is too thick, then return it to a clean pan and reheat. Add a swirl of single cream and serve.

Watercress soup

CALORIES PER PORTION 285 kCals

Watercress is simply bursting with vitamins and minerals. Make this soup when you have a cold to help you get back on your feet in no time.

SERVES 2 A GOOD BUNCH OF WATERCRESS, ABOUT 100 G (3½ OZ) | A SLIVER OF BUTTER, NO MORE THAN 10 G (½ OZ)
2 TEASPOONS SUNFLOWER OIL | 1 ONION, CHOPPED | 1 POTATO (ABOUT 100G), PEELED ANDCHOPPED
150 ML (5 FL OZ) VEGETABLE STOCK OR WATER | 250 ML (8 FL OZ) MILK | 2 TABLESPOONS SINGLE CREAM
SALT AND FRESHLY GROUND BLACK PEPPER | 2 TABLESPOONS LOW-FAT CRÈME FRAÎCHE, TO GARNISH

1. Roughly separate the watercress leaves from the stalks. Chop the stalks and set the whole leaves aside.

2. Put the butter and oil in a large heavy-based saucepan over a medium heat. When the butter has melted and started to bubble, add the onion. Cook it gently, stirring, for about 5–10 minutes, until softened but not brown.

3. Stir in the chopped potato and cook gently for a couple of minutes. Add a little stock to prevent it from sticking, if necessary. Then add the watercress stalks, the rest of the stock and the milk. Bring the soup to the boil, then reduce the temperature and simmer for about 10 minutes, or until the potato is tender.

4. Add the watercress leaves (save a few to use as a garnish) and simmer for a further minute or so. Transfer the soup to a food processor or blender and whizz until smooth.

5. Pour the soup into a clean saucepan, add the single cream and warm it through gently – do not let it boil. Check the seasoning, adding a little salt and pepper to taste. Serve with a tablespoon of crème fraîche dropped into each bowl and a few watercress leaves scattered on top.

Pea soup with mint

CALORIES PER PORTION without croutons: 250 kCals; with croutons: 380 kCals

Pea and mint is one of those classic combinations that frequently turns up on restaurant menus purely because it works so well!

SERVES 2 1 TEASPOON SUNFLOWER OR RAPESEED OIL | 1 SLIVER OF BUTTER, NOT MORE THAN 10 G (½ OZ)
1 ONION, FINELY CHOPPED | 400 G (13 OZ) FROZEN PEAS | WATER OR VEGETABLE STOCK, ABOUT 500 ML (17 FL OZ)
1 MINT SPRIG | 3 TABLESPOONS SINGLE CREAM | SALT AND FRESHLY GROUND BLACK PEPPER
SERVE WITH: 2 SLICES WHOLEMEAL BREAD AND 2 TEASPOONS OLIVE OIL (ONLY FOR THOSE ON PLANS B, C AND D)

1. Put the oil and butter in a large heavy-based saucepan over a medium heat. When the butter has melted and started to bubble, add the onion. Cook it gently, stirring, for about 5–10 minutes, until softened but not brown.

2. Put the frozen peas in a sieve and rinse under a cold tap to dislodge any excess ice, then add them to the pan. Stir in the peas until coated with butter, oil and onion, then add enough water or stock to cover – about 500 ml (17 fl oz).

3. Tear the smallest leaves off the mint sprig and add them to the soup, then drop in the whole sprig. Simmer the soup for about 20 minutes, or until the peas are soft.

4. When the soup is nearly ready, those on Plans B, C and D can make their croutons. Cut the slices of bread into cubes. Put the oil into a frying pan over a medium to high heat and, when it is hot, add the bread cubes. Flip them over and over until they are browned, then take them out of the pan and keep them warm while you finish the soup.

5. Remove the sprig of mint, transfer the soup to a food processor or blender and whizz until smooth. Return it to the pan, check for seasoning and add a little salt and black pepper to taste.

6. Add the single cream and warm the soup through – do not let it boil. Serve immediately, garnished with the croutons (if having).

Beetroot soup with yogurt

CALORIES PER PORTION 210 kCals

Fantastic colour and fantastic flavour. This is the Biggest Loser version of an Eastern European soup known as borscht.

SERVES 2 2 TEASPOONS OLIVE OIL | 1 SMALL ONION, CHOPPED | 4 RAW BEETROOT | 2 GARLIC CLOVES, CHOPPED
1 X 227 G (7½ OZ) CAN OF CHOPPED TOMATOES | A SMALL PINCH OF GROUND CUMIN
A SMALL PINCH OF GROUND CORIANDER | 350 ML (12 FL OZ) CHICKEN STOCK OR WATER
SALT AND FRESHLY GROUND BLACK PEPPER

SERVE WITH: 150 G (5 OZ) NATURAL YOGURT AND A HANDFUL OF FRESH CHIVES

1. Heat the oil in a heavy-based saucepan over a medium heat, and add the onion. Cook gently for about 5 minutes, until softened but not brown.

2. Meanwhile, prepare the beetroot. Trim and peel them, then chop them up. This is best done on a china or glass plate because the juice can stain worktops or chopping boards.

3. Add the beetroot to the saucepan. Then add the garlic and stir everything together well and cook for a further 5 minutes.

4. Add the tomatoes, cumin and coriander. Add the stock or water and bring the soup to a simmer. Cook until the beetroot is tender, about 20 minutes.

5. Take the pan off the heat and check the soup for seasoning. Transfer the soup to a food processor or blender and whizz until smooth. Reheat if necessary, or serve immediately if the soup is still hot enough. Decorate each bowl with a generous swirl of yogurt, and snip chives over the top.

Smooth leek & potato soup

CALORIES PER PORTION 160 kCals,

This old favourite is also delicious served cold. It's good with a tablespoon of single cream swirled in before serving, which would only add an extra 30 calories.

SERVES 4 2 TEASPOONS OLIVE OIL | 1 KG (2 LB) LEEKS, TRIMMED, CLEANED AND SLICED
400 G (13 OZ) POTATOES, PEELED AND CHOPPED | A THYME SPRIG OR A PINCH OF DRIED THYME
VEGETABLE STOCK OR WATER | 200 ML (7 FL OZ) SKIMMED MILK | SALT AND WHITE PEPPER

1. Heat the oil in a large, heavy-based saucepan over a medium heat. Add the leeks and cook them gently for about 5 minutes – keep an eye on them and don't let them brown.

2. Add the potatoes, the leaves from the thyme sprig and enough stock or water to cover the vegetables– about 500 ml (17 fl oz). Cover the saucepan and simmer for 15–20 minutes.

3 Add the milk and cook for a further 20 minutes. Check the soup for seasoning, add salt and pepper to taste, then remove the saucepan from the heat.

4. Allow the soup to cool a little, then transfer to a food processor or blender and whizz until smooth. Adjust the thickness of the soup by adding a little more liquid if it seems necessary (if you want your soup to be completely smoth, pass it through a sieve using a wooden spoon). Return it to a clean pan and reheat. Serve immediately.

Cauliflower soup with a choice of toppings

CALORIES PER PORTION without a garnish: 175 kCals; with topping 1: 205 kCals;
with topping 2: 215 kCals; with topping 3: 225 kCals

Choose from three different garnishes to add texture and extra flavour to this rather special soup.

SERVES 2, GENEROUSLY 1 TEASPOON SUNFLOWER OIL | 1 ONION, CHOPPED | 1 SMALL CAULIFLOWER
1 GARLIC CLOVE, CHOPPED | 100 G (3½ OZ) POTATO, PEELED AND CHOPPED
VEGETABLE STOCK, JUST ENOUGH TO COVER, ABOUT 600 ML (1 PINT) | SALT AND FRESHLY GROUND BLACK PEPPER
FOR TOPPING 1: 2 TABLESPOONS NATURAL YOGURT AND A SPRINKLE OF CHOPPED FLAT-LEAF PARSLEY
FOR TOPPING 2: A FEW ALMOND FLAKES THAT HAVE BEEN TOASTED IN A DRY FRYING PAN
FOR TOPPING 3: HALF A SLICE OF WHOLEMEAL BREAD, TOASTED, LIGHTLY RUBBED WITH GARLIC AND CUT INTO CROUTONS

1. Heat the oil in a heavy-based saucepan over a medium heat, and add the onion. Cook gently for about 5 minutes, until softened but not brown. While the onion is cooking, prepare the cauliflower, removing the outer leaves and stem and cutting it into medium to small florets.

2. Add the garlic to the pan when the onions are nearly ready and warm it through. Then add the cauliflower, the potato and enough stock to cover the vegetables. Bring to the boil, then reduce the heat and simmer until the potatoes are soft.

3. Remove from the heat, leave to cool slightly and adjust the seasoning if necessary. Transfer the soup to a food processor or blender and whizz until smooth, adding a little boiling water to thin it down if necessary. Return the soup to the pan, reheat and serve with your choice of topping.

Italian winter bean soup

CALORIES PER PORTION 175 kCals

This warming Italian soup is traditionally made in advance and reheated once the family is seated round the table. It freezes really well, which makes it a great make-ahead soup.

SERVES 4 1 TABLESPOON OLIVE OIL | 1 LARGE RED ONION, CHOPPED | 2 CELERY STICKS, CHOPPED
1 LARGE CARROT, CHOPPED | 2 GARLIC CLOVES, CHOPPED | 1 X 400 G (13 OZ) CAN OF CHOPPED TOMATOES, DRAINED
750 G (1½ LB) BLACK KALE (*CAVOLO NERO*) OR THE DARKEST LEAVES FROM A SAVOY CABBAGE, FINELY CHOPPED
1 X 400 G (13 OZ) CAN OF BORLOTTI BEANS, DRAINED AND RINSED | SALT AND FRESHLY GROUND BLACK PEPPER

1. Heat the oil in a large, heavy-based saucepan or ovenproof casserole over a medium heat and add the onion, celery and carrot. Cook the vegetables gently, stirring now and then, until softened, but not brown, about 5–10 minutes.

2. Add the garlic and cook for 5 more minutes. Then add the tomatoes, breaking them up, and cook for a further 10 minutes. Finally add the kale or cabbage, half the borlotti beans and enough water to cover the vegetables.

3. Simmer the soup for about 30 minutes. If it looks as though the liquid may be disappearing during this time, add a little more. The soup should be thick, but it shouldn't catch on the bottom of the pan.

4. Crush the rest of the beans with a fork, and stir them into the soup to thicken. Check the water level and add boiling water if necessary. Season with salt and black pepper to taste. Serve immediately.

Black bean soup with celery

CALORIES PER PORTION 155 kCals

Hearty and filling, with just a hint of spice, this is great served from a flask for a working lunch.

SERVES 4 150 G (5 OZ) DRIED BLACK BEANS, SOAKED OVERNIGHT | 750 ML (1¼ PINTS) WATER | 1 ONION, CHOPPED
1 GARLIC CLOVE, FINELY CHOPPED | 5 CELERY STICKS, CHOPPED (INCLUDING THE LEAVES) | 1 BAY LEAF
½ TEASPOON CAYENNE PEPPER | SALT AND FRESHLY GROUND BLACK PEPPER

1. Drain and rinse the soaked beans. Put them in a saucepan, cover with water and bring to the boil. Cook at a hard boil for 10 minutes, skimming away any froth that forms, then remove from the heat. Drain and rinse the beans.

2. Put the beans in a large saucepan and add the measured water. Add the onion, garlic, celery, bay leaf and cayenne and bring to the boil. Reduce the heat and simmer for 1–1½ hours until the

beans are soft (how long this takes will depend on how fresh they are).

3. Find the bay leaf and remove it, then transfer the soup to a food processor or blender and whizz until smooth, adding a little water to thin it down if necessary. Return the soup to a clean pan, reheat and season with salt and black pepper to taste. Serve immediately.

Refreshing Chinese vegetable soup with prawns

CALORIES PER PORTION 90 kCals

Make this with 150 g (5 oz) cold cooked chicken instead of prawns, if you prefer. If you use white chicken meat, it would only be 15 calories more.

SERVES 1 1.25 LITRES (2 PINTS) FRESH CHICKEN STOCK
A 2 CM (JUST UNDER 1 INCH) CUBE OF FRESH ROOT GINGER, PEELED AND GRATED | 1 GARLIC CLOVE, CRUSHED
10 SPRING ONIONS, CHOPPED (INCLUDING SOME OF THE GREEN STALK) | 12 MUSHROOMS, FINELY SLICED
100 G (3½ OZ) CHINESE LEAVES OR PAK CHOI, FINELY SLICED | 150 G (5 OZ) COOKED SHELLED PRAWNS

1. Put the stock in a large saucepan over a medium heat and bring to the boil. Reduce the heat slightly and add the ginger, garlic and spring onions. Simmer for 5 minutes.

2. Add the mushrooms and Chinese leaves or pak choi. Simmer for a further minute and add the prawns. Cook for 2 more minutes and then serve immediately.

VARIATION: To make 'egg-flower soup', whisk 3 eggs in a bowl and, just before serving the soup as above, pour them into the soup in a steady stream. Do not stir; just remove from the heat and check the seasoning before dishing up the soup (this adds 160 calories per portion)

Dhal with chapatti and raita

CALORIES PER PORTION for the dhal: 390 kCals; with the raita: 455 kCals: with the raita
and the chapatti or pitta: 530 kCals

Indian food is full of flavour and very healthy when it's home-cooked without the vast quantities of oil some Indian restaurants use.

SERVES 2 175 G (6 OZ) RED LENTILS OR YELLOW SPLIT PEAS, RINSED AND DRAINED | 1 TEASPOON SUNFLOWER OIL
1 SMALL ONION, FINELY CHOPPED | A 2 CM (JUST UNDER 1 INCH) PIECE OF FRESH ROOT GINGER, PEELED AND GRATED
1 GARLIC CLOVE, FINELY CHOPPED | ½ TEASPOON TURMERIC | 1 TEASPOON GARAM MASALA
2 TABLESPOONS DESICCATED COCONUT
FOR THE RAITA: A QUARTER OF A CUCUMBER | 150 G (5 OZ) LOW-FAT NATURAL YOGURT | A PINCH OF GROUND CUMIN
SERVE WITH: 2 CHAPATTI (SEE BOX) OR HALF A STANDARD WHOLEMEAL
PITTA BREAD PER SERVING

1. Put the lentils in a saucepan with enough water to cover, about 400 ml (14 fl oz). Bring to the boil, skimming off any froth that forms and then reduce the temperature to a simmer. Cook until the lentils begin to soften and break up; this will probably take about 35 minutes, but will depend on how fresh the lentils are. They will absorb a lot of the water as they cook, so keep an eye on them and stir to make sure they don't stick. They should be moist and not bone dry; if there is still too much water left once the lentils are ready, increase the heat and cook it off.

2. While the lentils cook, make the raita. Grate the cucumber into a bowl, then squeeze it over the sink to get most of the liquid out, and transfer to a clean bowl. Add the yogurt and the cumin, stir well and put in the fridge to chill a little.

3. When the lentils are almost cooked, put the oil in a small non-stick frying pan over a medium heat. Add the onion and cook for 5 minutes, then add the ginger and garlic and cook for a further minute. Add the turmeric and garam masala and stir to warm through, then add the coconut. Stir everything well, and remove from the heat.

4. Add the onion, spice and coconut mix to the lentils, and stir everything together. Transfer to a serving dish and serve, accompanied with the raita and chapatti or pitta.

B Add another tablespoon desiccated coconut (this adds 90 calories)

C Add more coconut, as for B, and have a whole pitta bread as well or double the chapatti ingredients and have 4 per serving (this adds 165 calories)

D As for C, and also make the dhal with 225 g (7½ oz) lentils and a medium onion as well (this adds 255 calories)

Chapatti

MAKES 4 50 G (2 OZ) PLAIN WHOLEMEAL FLOUR | 1 TABLESPOON WATER

1. Put the flour in a bowl and add the water gradually, mixing them together until they form a dough. Knead on a lightly floured worktop for 10 minutes, then put it back in the bowl, cover and set aside for 30 minutes – but don't put it in the fridge; keep it warm.

2. Knead the dough again and divide it into 4 pieces; form these pieces into small balls. Heat a dry frying pan, and flour a worktop while it heats. Roll out the first ball of dough on the worktop, turning it round and over to make a circle of bread about 10–12 cm (4–5 inches) in diameter.

3. Shake any excess flour off the chapatti and put it straight in the dry pan. When the upper side begins to bubble – after about 20–30 seconds – flip it over and cook the other side. This should take even less time. Cook the rest and serve immediately.

South indian potato curry

CALORIES PER PORTION for the curry: 300 kCals; for the curry and the raita: 385 kCals

If you have a microwave in the office, take a portion of this to work for a satisfying lunch that gives you energy for the whole afternoon.

SERVES 2 600 G (1 LB 3 OZ) POTATOES, PEELED AND CHOPPED INTO 2 CM (JUST UNDER 1 INCH) CHUNKS
1 TABLESPOON SUNFLOWER OIL | 1 ONION, FINELY CHOPPED | 1 FAT GARLIC CLOVE, FINELY CHOPPED
½ TEASPOON GROUND CUMIN | ½ TEASPOON GARAM MASALA
1–2 RED CHILLIES, TO TASTE, DESEEDED AND VERY FINELY CHOPPED | A SMALL PINCH OF TURMERIC
50–100 ML (2–3½ FL OZ) WATER | SALT

SERVE WITH: 1 QUANTITY RAITA (SEE PAGE 98)

1. Put a saucepan of water over a medium to high heat, add the potato and cook at a high simmer for about 10 minutes, until the potato chunks are almost tender. If they show signs of being cooked more quickly, take them off the heat. Drain and set aside.

2. Heat the oil in a large saucepan with a lid, and add the onion and garlic. Cook for about 5 minutes.

3. Add the cumin, garam masala and chillies and stir everything together. Cook for a further minute, then put the drained potatoes in the pan with a little bit of salt and the turmeric. Stir, add the water and then cover the pan and let the potatoes cook in the steam for about 5 minutes (check that they're not drying out and catching, and add a little more water if necessary).

4. This should be a rather dry curry, so make sure that most of the liquid has evaporated before serving; if not, cook it on a slightly higher heat for 1–2 minutes. Serve the curry with the raita.

B Have half a standard wholemeal pitta or 2 chapatti (see page 98), warmed in the oven, and some spinach on the side (wash and put it in a pan over a medium heat until it wilts, then drain off excess liquid) as well (this adds 85 calories)

C Have a whole standard wholemeal pitta bread and some spinach, as for B (this adds 160 calories)

D Have a whole pitta bread and some spinach, as for C, but make the raita with 300 g (10 oz) yogurt (this adds 205 calories)

Ratatouille with roast chicken breast

CALORIES PER PORTION for the ratatouille: 100 kCals; for the chicken: 150 kCals

This dish freezes beautifully. It's worth cooking in bulk and freezing in individual portions so you always have a nutritious meal on standby.

SERVES 4 1 TABLESPOON OLIVE OIL | 1 LARGE ONION, CHOPPED | 2 GARLIC CLOVES
1 GREEN PEPPER, DESEEDED AND CHOPPED | 1 AUBERGINE, CHOPPED INTO 2 CM (JUST UNDER 1 INCH) CUBES
1 LARGE COURGETTE, CHOPPED | 1 X 400 G (13 OZ) CAN OF CHOPPED TOMATOES
PINCH OF DRIED HERBES DE PROVENCE (OR MIXED HERBS) | SALT AND FRESHLY GROUND BLACK PEPPER
4 X LARGE SKINLESS CHICKEN BREASTS, WEIGHING ABOUT 125 G (4 OZ) EACH
1 TABLESPOON OLIVE OIL

SERVE WITH: A MIXED GREEN SALAD

1. Preheat the oven to 200°C (400°F) Gas mark 6, and prepare the ratatouille. Warm the olive oil in a large, heavy-based saucepan or casserole over a medium heat, then add the onions and cook for about 15 minutes, or until they are soft and transparent. Don't let them burn; if they show signs of catching, add a little water.

2. Stir in the garlic, green pepper and aubergine and cook for a further 10 minutes. Add the courgette, tomato and herbs. Check the seasoning, and add salt and pepper to taste. Simmer over a gentle heat, stirring regularly, until the sauce is thick and all the vegetables are soft – this will take about 35 minutes.

3. When the ratatouille has about 20–25 minutes to go, prepare the chicken breasts. Put the olive oil in an ovenproof dish, rinse the fillets and pat them dry, then turn them in the oil so they are evenly coated. Put the dish in the preheated oven and roast for 15 minutes, then turn them over and cook for a further 5 minutes. Check that they are done, which will depend on their size – a knife inserted in the thickest part of the fillet should produce a little clear liquid. If they are ready, flip them back over and return them to the oven while you dish up the ratatouille (if not, the ratatouille can continue cooking until they are). Serve, accompanied by a green salad.

B Have 150 g (5 oz) boiled new potatoes as well (this adds 115 calories)

C Have a portion of boiled rice, with a dry weight of 50 g (2 oz) as well (this adds 180 calories)

D Have a portion of boiled rice, as for C, and also dress the green salad with vinaigrette (see page 43) (this adds 215 calories)

Greek bean stew

CALORIES PER PORTION 200 kCals

This hearty Mediterranean dish ticks all the boxes: it's tasty, filling and full of goodness.

SERVES 4 3 X 400 G (13 OZ) CANS OF BUTTER BEANS, DRAINED AND RINSED | 1 TABLESPOON OLIVE OIL
2 ONIONS, CHOPPED | 2 CELERY STICKS, FINELY CHOPPED | 2 CARROTS, CHOPPED | 2 GARLIC CLOVES, FINELY CHOPPED
1 TEASPOON MIXED DRIED HERBS | 1 X 400 G (13 OZ) CAN OF CHOPPED TOMATOES | 1 COURGETTE, CHOPPED
2 TEASPOONS TOMATO PURÉE | 2 TEASPOONS CLEAR HONEY | SALT AND FRESHLY GROUND BLACK PEPPER

SERVE WITH: A GREEN SALAD

1. Put the butter beans in a saucepan and cover with water. Bring to the boil and cook for about 1 minute – don't let them disintegrate. Remove the pan from the heat, drain and rinse the beans.

2. Preheat the oven to 180°C (350°F) Gas mark 4. Warm the olive oil in a large saucepan over a medium heat. Add the onions and cook for 5–10 minutes, or until they begin to change colour, then stir in the celery, carrots and garlic and cook for a further 2 minutes.

3. Add the herbs, chopped tomatoes and courgette. Fill the empty tomato can with water, mix in the tomato purée and swirl the liquid around to collect any remaining tomato juice, then tip it into the pan. Cook for a further 10 minutes.

4. Add the beans and the honey; stir well and cook for a further 5 minutes. Check the seasoning and add salt and pepper to taste. Ladle the bean and vegetable mixture into a large ovenproof dish. Bake in the preheated oven for 30–40 minutes, until the beans on the surface start to get crispy (check the stew during the cooking time and add a little water if it looks too dry). Remove the dish from the oven and serve, accompanied by a plain green salad.

B Add a dressing to the salad (2 teaspoons olive oil and ½ teaspoon balsamic vinegar) as well (this adds 85 calories)

C Add salad dressing, as for B, and have a 50 g (2 oz) piece of ciabatta or similar bread (no spread) as well (this adds 220 calories)

D Add salad dressing, as for B, and have a small individual ciabatta, about 85 g (3¼ oz) as well (this adds 315 calories)

Tunisian fish stew with couscous

CALORIES PER PORTION 325 kCals

Cod fillet can be substituted for the monkfish, but add it later in the cooking time as it is usually thinner and will disintegrate if overcooked.

SERVES 4 1 X PIECE OF MONKFISH TAIL, WEIGHING ABOUT 500 G (1 LB) | 2 TEASPOONS OLIVE OIL
2 ONIONS, FINELY CHOPPED | 2 GARLIC CLOVES, CHOPPED | 1 TEASPOON GROUND CUMIN
½ TEASPOON CAYENNE PEPPER | ½ TEASPOON TURMERIC | 2 CARROTS, PEELED AND CHOPPED
2 RED PEPPERS, DESEEDED AND CHOPPED | 12 SMALL NEW POTATOES, NOT MORE THAN 250 G (8 OZ)
4 TEASPOONS TOMATO PURÉE DISSOLVED IN 400 ML (14 FL OZ) HOT WATER | 200 G (7 OZ) COUSCOUS

1. Fillet the monkfish. Using a really sharp knife, slice the fillets away from the central bone, then cut away the purplish membrane on the outside. Discard the bone and membrane, cut the flesh into chunks, put them in a bowl, cover and set aside.

2. Put the oil in a large saucepan over a medium heat. Add the onions and cook for 5 minutes until softened but not brown. Add the garlic and stir in the spices, and cook for a further minute, stirring well. Put the carrot, peppers and potatoes in the pan, mix them in, then add the tomato purée and water. Cook for 15 minutes.

3. Add the monkfish. Top up with some more water to cover everything, if necessary – this fish stew should be quite liquid. Partly cover the pan and cook for a further 10 minutes, or until both the vegetables and the monkfish are cooked and the liquid has reduced a little.

4. Towards the end of the cooking time, prepare the couscous. Boil a kettle and put the couscous in a large bowl. Cover it well with boiling water and stir with a fork. Cover the bowl with a saucepan lid, and wait until the grains have plumped up and absorbed a lot of the water (add more if you need to) – about 2 minutes. Stir the couscous a couple of times, then drain it well through a fine sieve if necessary.

5. Put a serving of couscous on each plate and ladle the stew over it. Serve immediately.

B Have a rocket salad dressed with 1 teaspoon olive oil and drizzled with a little lemon juice as well (this adds 50 calories)

C Have a salad, as for B, increase the couscous to 240 g (7¾ oz) and have a piece of wholemeal bread to mop up any remaining sauce as well (this adds 175 calories)

D Have a salad and a piece of bread, as for C, but increase the couscous to 300 g (10 oz) (this adds 225 calories)

Chicken, bacon & mushroom stew

CALORIES PER PORTION 475 kCals

This is a version of the French dish known as 'Coq au vin', but without any fiddly bones to fish out of the stew.

SERVES 4 600 G (1 LB 3 OZ) SKINLESS CHICKEN BREASTS, CUT INTO LARGE CHUNKS | 2 TEASPOONS PLAIN FLOUR
2 TABLESPOONS OLIVE OIL | 2 LEAN BACK BACON RASHERS, CHOPPED INTO STRIPS
100 G (3½ OZ) SMALL ONIONS, PEELED AND LARGER ONES HALVED | 2 GARLIC CLOVES, FINELY CHOPPED
150 ML (¼ PINT) RED WINE | 250 G (8 OZ) MUSHROOMS, CHOPPED, INCLUDING STALKS
500–600 ML (17–20 FL OZ) FRESH CHICKEN STOCK OR WATER | 1 BAY LEAF | 1 THYME SPRIG
SALT AND FRESHLY GROUND BLACK PEPPER

FOR THE MASHED POTATOES: 300 G (10 OZ) POTATOES, PEELED AND CHOPPED | 10 G (½ OZ) BUTTER
2 TEASPOONS SEMI-SKIMMED MILK

SERVE WITH: 200 G (7 OZ) BROCCOLI

1. Put the chicken breasts in a bowl, sprinkle the flour over them and then mix to evenly cover. Put 1 teaspoon of oil in a large pan or heatproof casserole and set over a medium heat, then add the chicken pieces and seal, turning them over. Remove the chicken from the pan and set it aside.

2. Add the remaining oil to the pan and add the bacon, onions and garlic. Stir them until they begin to brown, then add a quick slug of the wine to stop them sticking. Cook for 2 minutes and then add the mushrooms and another slug of wine. Cook for 2 further minutes.

3. Return the chicken to the pan and stir well. Add the rest of the wine and the chicken stock or water to cover. Bring to the boil, then reduce the heat to a steady simmer and cook until the chicken is tender, about 45 minutes.

4. When the stew is nearly ready, prepare the vegetables. Put the potatoes in a saucepan of cold water. Bring to the boil and cook until the potatoes are tender. Boil the broccoli in a separate pan until it is tender. Drain the potatoes, then add the butter, milk, a little salt and black pepper, and mash them well.

5. Check the seasoning of the stew and serve, accompanied by the mashed potato and the broccoli.

B Have a green salad dressed with 2 teaspoons olive oil and 1 teaspoon wine vinegar as well (this adds 90 calories)

C Have a salad, as for B, and a larger portion of mash (make it with 400 g/13 oz potatoes, a tiny bit more butter and another teaspoon of milk), and also have a small 150 ml (¼ pint) glass of red wine (this adds 240 calories)

D As for C, and have a larger serving of the stew (consider this as serving 3 people rather than 4) as well (this adds 340 calories).

Fish, Poultry
& Meat

Haddock, baby vegetables & mayonnaise with a hint of garlic

CALORIES PER PORTION 455 kCals

Use any baby vegetables you like for this tasty supper dish with Mediterranean-style mayo.

SERVES 2 5 TABLESPOONS LIGHT MAYONNAISE | A SQUEEZE OF LEMON JUICE | 2 GARLIC CLOVES, CRUSHED
2 X HADDOCK FILLETS, WEIGHING ABOUT 200 G (7 OZ) EACH | 1 LARGE ONION, CUT INTO LARGE CHUNKS
1 LARGE CARROT, CUT INTO LARGE CHUNKS | 1 THYME SPRIG | 250 G (8 OZ) SMALL NEW POTATOES
150 G (5 OZ) BABY CARROTS, TRIMMED | 50 G (2 OZ) MANGETOUT, TRIMMED, OR PEAS
100 G (3½ OZ) SMALL GREEN BEANS, TOPPED AND TAILED
A SLIVER OF BUTTER, NOT MORE THAN 10 G (½ OZ) | SALT

1. To prepare the mayonnaise, put the mayonnaise, lemon juice and garlic in a bowl and mix well. Cover with clingfilm and refrigerate until needed.

2. Wipe the haddock fillets clean, run them briefly under the tap to rinse, then pat them dry with kitchen paper and place in a shallow dish. Sprinkle with a little salt, cover and put in the fridge to chill until needed.

3. Put the onion, carrot and thyme in a saucepan and cover with plenty of water. Bring to the boil and simmer for 10 minutes, then strain out the vegetables and pour the liquid into a frying pan large enough to hold the fish.

4. Put the new potatoes in a saucepan of lightly salted water and bring to the boil. Fill another saucepan with water, and put it over a medium heat. Add the baby carrots to this pan after the potatoes have been cooking for 5 minutes, and cook for a further 2 minutes. Then add the mangetout or peas and green beans and cook until all the vegetables are tender, about a further 5–7 minutes.

5. Meanwhile, put the frying pan with the liquid over a medium heat and bring it to a simmer. Carefully slip the fish into the liquid and simmer until the fillets are cooked – how long this takes will depend on how thick they are, but should be about 2–5 minutes. The flesh will be opaque and flake easily when the fish is ready.

6. Drain the vegetables and put them in a warmed serving bowl; add a sliver of butter. Lift the fish out of the liquid using a slotted fish slice and put on warmed plates. Serve immediately with the baby vegetables, and with the garlic mayonnaise on the side.

B Have a slice of wholemeal bread with 1 teaspoon low-fat spread as well (this adds 100 calories)

C Have half a wholemeal roll with 1 teaspoon low-fat spread and add 1 more tablespoon mayonnaise as well (this adds 185 calories)

D Have an entire wholemeal roll with 2 teaspoons low-fat spread and add 1 more tablespoon mayonnaise as well (this adds 325 calories)

Baked mackerel with carrot & fennel salad

CALORIES PER PORTION 590 Cals

If you never buy fennel because you're not sure how to cook it,
try simply slicing it raw, as in this delicious salad.

SERVES 2 2 X WHOLE FRESH MACKEREL (CLEANED AND HEADS REMOVED), WEIGHING ABOUT 200 G (7 OZ) EACH
2 LEMONS | A BUNCH OF FLAT-LEAF PARSLEY, LEAVES ONLY | 1 LARGE SHALLOT OR SMALL ONION, SLICED
2 GARLIC CLOVES, HALVED | 300 G (10 OZ) NEW POTATOES | 3 CARROTS, GRATED | 1 FENNEL BULB, VERY FINELY SLICED
4 TEASPOONS OLIVE OIL | 2 TEASPOONS WHITE WINE VINEGAR 15 G (¾ OZ) BUTTER
SALT AND FRESHLY GROUND BLACK PEPPER

1. Preheat the oven to 200°C (400°F), Gas mark 6. Wipe the fish clean, run them briefly under the cold tap to rinse, then pat them dry with kitchen paper. Put them on 2 large squares of foil and season them, inside and out.

2. Slice one lemon and stuff the fish with the slices, then add the parsley, the onion and the garlic halves. Pull the foil up around the fish and squeeze the juice of the other lemon all over the fish. Bring the foil up and seal the parcels. Carefully transfer them to a roasting dish and bake in the preheated oven for 25 minutes.

3. Meanwhile, prepare the potatoes and the salad. Put the potatoes into a pan of lightly salted cold water, bring to the boil and cook until they are tender. Mix the carrot and fennel in a large bowl. Put the oil and vinegar in a jar, add a little black pepper, then seal the jar and shake until the dressing has combined. Pour it over the carrot and fennel and stir well. Drain the potatoes, put them in a bowl and slice the butter over the top.

4. Take the mackerel out of the oven and carefully unwrap the parcels. Put a fish on each plate and serve with the salad and new potatoes in their separate serving dishes.

B Increase the amount of potatoes to 500 g (1 lb) between two people (this adds 75 calories)

C Increase the amount of potatoes, as for B, and have half a wholemeal roll with 1 teaspoon low-fat spread as well (this adds 215 calories)

D As for B, and have an entire wholemeal roll with 2 teaspoons low-fat spread as well (this adds 355 calories)

Tuna with Mexican salsa

CALORIES PER PORTION 396 kCals

Tuna has a satisfyingly meaty texture, and it is great served with this tangy salsa, which can be as mild or as fiery as you like.

SERVES 2   4 RIPE TOMATOES | 1 JALAPENO, OR 3 HOT GREEN CHILLIES (OR TO TASTE)
1 SMALL ONION | A SMALL BUNCH OF FRESH CORIANDER, LEAVES ONLY | JUICE OF 1 LIME
2 TABLESPOONS OLIVE OIL | 2 X FRESH TUNA STEAKS, WEIGHING ABOUT 150 G (5 OZ) EACH
SALT AND FRESHLY GROUND BLACK PEPPER

SERVE WITH: SALAD LEAVES

1. To make the salsa, finely chop the tomatoes, chilli and onion, being very careful to wash your hands after chopping the chillies (it is best not to do this in a food processor or blender as the salsa vegetables should be finely chopped, not pulverized). Put them in a bowl.

2. Finely chop the coriander leaves and add them to the bowl. Squeeze in the lime juice and season with a little salt. Mix everything together thoroughly, then cover the bowl with clingfilm and chill the salsa in the fridge for at least 30 minutes.

3. Put the oil in a frying pan over a high heat. Sprinkle the tuna steaks with a little salt, then put them in the pan when the oil is very hot. Cook for no more than 2 minutes before turning them over. How long they take will depend on their thickness; check by cutting into one steak with a sharp knife. Part the cut slightly and see how pink they are inside – tuna is best served rare and should be slightly pink, but cook it to taste. Just be careful not to overcook it, or it will be tough.

4. Season and serve immediately with the salsa on the side and accompanied by a green salad.

B Have a portion of healthy chips using a 175 g (6 oz) potato (see page 150) as well (this adds 170 calories)

C As for B, but use a 200 g (7 oz) potato and add a dressing to the green salad (1 teaspoon olive oil and a sprinkling of lime juice) as well (this adds 230 calories)

D As for C, but have larger tuna steaks, about 200 g (7 oz) each, as well (this adds 315 calories).

Baked cod with a crispy tomato crust

CALORIES PER PORTION 460 kCal

If you're used to batter on your cod, you're in for a pleasant surprise,
because this version with a crispy crust is much tastier.

SERVES 2 2 X COD LOINS, WEIGHING ABOUT 175 G (6 OZ) EACH | 1 TABLESPOON OLIVE OIL, PLUS EXTRA FOR GREASING
1 SLICE OF WHOLEMEAL BREAD (STALE IS FINE) OR 1 TABLESPOON FRESH BREADCRUMBS
2 RIPE TOMATOES, DESEEDED AND VERY FINELY CHOPPED | 1 SMALL RED ONION, VERY FINELY CHOPPED
1 GARLIC CLOVE, FINELY CHOPPED (OPTIONAL) | A THYME SPRIG | 300 G (10 OZ) NEW POTATOES
A SLIVER OF BUTTER, NOT MORE THAN 10 G (½ OZ) IN TOTAL | SALT AND FRESHLY GROUND BLACK PEPPER
SERVE WITH: SALAD LEAVES

1. Preheat the oven to 200°C (400°F) Gas mark
6. Wipe the cod loins clean, run them briefly
under the tap to rinse, then pat them dry with
kitchen paper. Line a large baking tin with foil,
lightly oil the foil and put the pieces of fish on it,
skin side down.

2. Put the slice of bread in a food processor or
blender and whizz it into breadcrumbs. Empty
them into a bowl and add the tomatoes, onion
and garlic. Add the thyme leaves and stir in the
olive oil. Season with salt and pepper and stir
everything together well.

3. Pile the tomato mixture on top of the pieces
of fish, spreading it out as evenly as possible.
Put the fish in the preheated oven and bake
until done – when the flesh is opaque and flakes
easily – which will take about 10–15 minutes,
depending on the thickness of the loins.

4. Meanwhile, put the potatoes into a pan of
lightly salted cold water, bring to the boil and cook
until they are tender. As soon as the fish is ready,
lift it carefully off the foil and onto plates. Serve
immediately, with the boiled potatoes with a little
butter on them and a green salad.

B Increase the amount
of potatoes to 400 g (13 oz)
between 2 servings and add a
dressing to the salad (2 teaspoons
olive oil and 1 teaspoon lemon
juice) as well (this adds 130
calories)

C Increase the amount
of potatoes and add a salad
dressing, as for B, and have
1 tablespoon light mayonnaise
on the side as well (this adds 175
calories)

D As for B, but increase the
amount of potatoes to 500 g
(1 lb) for 2 servings and have
2 tablespoons light mayonnaise
on the side (this adds 260
calories)

Salmon with yellow pepper, tomato & onion

CALORIES PER PORTION 565 kCals

This colourful dish is basically salmon with its own salsa on top,
and it tastes every bit as good as it looks.

SERVES 2 2 x SALMON FILLETS, WEIGHING ABOUT 125 G (4 OZ) EACH | JUICE OF 2 LEMONS, PLUS 2 LEMON SLICES
2 TEASPOONS OLIVE OIL | 1 GARLIC CLOVE, CRUSHED | 1 BUNCH OF FLAT-LEAF PARSLEY, LEAVES ONLY
1 YELLOW PEPPER, DESEEDED AND FINELY CHOPPED | 3 RIPE TOMATOES, QUARTERED, DESEEDED AND FINELY CHOPPED
1 SMALL RED ONION, CUT IN HALF AND FINELY SLICED | ½ TEASPOON SUGAR
SALT AND FRESHLY GROUND BLACK PEPPER

SERVE WITH: BOILED RICE, MADE WITH 100 G (3½ OZ) DRY LONG-GRAIN RICE, AND SALAD LEAVES

1. Wipe the salmon fillets clean, run them briefly under the cold tap to rinse, then pat them dry with kitchen paper.

2. Whisk the juice of 1 lemon together with the olive oil in a bowl, then add the garlic and whisk again. Put this mixture in a dish just large enough to take the two salmon fillets, and roll them over in it coat them. Cover with clingfilm and leave in the fridge to marinate for at least 2 hours (but no more than 10 hours).

3. Preheat the oven to 200°C (400°F) Gas mark 6. Take a large sheet of foil, big enough to wrap both salmon fillets in, and lift the salmon out of the dish and onto the foil. Spoon any remaining marinade around them and put a slice of lemon on top of each one. Bring the foil up around the fillets and seal it into a parcel. Carefully transfer the parcel to an ovenproof dish or baking sheet and bake in the preheated oven for 10 minutes.

4. Meanwhile, put the rice on to boil and prepare the vegetables. Chop the parsley leaves very finely, put them in a bowl and add the pepper, tomatos and red onion. Mix the sugar with the juice of the remaining lemon in a small bowl until it has dissolved, and then pour it over the pepper and tomato mixture. Add a little salt and black pepper and set to one side.

5. Take the fish out of the oven and carefully open the parcel, exposing the top of the salmon; push the lemon slices to one side. Put it back in the oven for 5 minutes or until the fish is cooked right through, then remove from the oven.

6. Drain the rice and divide it between 2 plates. Put a piece of salmon on top, add some of the juice from the foil and spoon the pepper and tomato mix on top and alongside. Serve immediately, accompanied by a green salad.

B Add a dressing to the salad (2 teaspoons olive oil and 1 teapoon balsamic vinegar) (this adds 90 calories)

C Add a salad dressing, as for B, and increase the amount of rice to 150 g (5 oz) between two servings as well (this adds 180 calories)

D Add a salad dressing, as for B, and have 3 salmon fillets between two servings (they may need a little extra cooking time) instead of 2 (this adds 225 calories)

Grilled salmon with ginger & lime butter

CALORIES PER PORTION 515 kCals

Use real butter rather than a low-fat alternative, but measure the amount exactly to keep the calories under control.

SERVES 2 200 G (7 OZ) NEW POTATOES, HALVED IF LARGER THAN 3 CM (1¼ INCH) LONG
25 G (1 OZ) BUTTER, SOFTENED | JUICE OF 2 LIMES
A 2 CM (JUST UNDER 1 INCH) PIECE OF FRESH ROOT GINGER, PEELED AND GRATED
2 X SALMON FILLETS, WEIGHING ABOUT 125 G (4 OZ) EACH | 2 TEASPOONS OLIVE OIL
100 G (3⅓ OZ) MANGETOUT | SALT AND FRESHLY GROUND BLACK PEPPER

1. Preheat the grill to high and put a saucepan of lightly salted water over a high heat. As soon as the water boils, add the potatoes and cook them until they are just tender (about 12–15 minutes).

2. Meanwhile, put the butter in a small bowl and squeeze the lime juice into it, mixing them together well with a spoon. Add the ginger and mix again; cover and set aside until needed.

3. Wipe the salmon fillets clean, run them briefly under the cold tap to rinse, then pat them dry with kitchen paper. Put the olive oil in a heatproof dish and turn the fillets in it to coat them, leaving them upside-down. Put the dish under the hot grill for 5 minutes, then turn the fillets over and use a knife to smear some of the lime and ginger butter on top of each fillet. Put back under the grill for a further 5 minutes or so, until the fillets are cooked right through. The fish should be opaque and flake easily.

4. Boil the mangetout in a separate saucepan for 3–4 minutes.

5. Drain the potatoes and put them on warmed serving plates. Put any remaining lime and ginger butter on top of the potatoes to melt, and carefully lift the salmon fillets onto the plates. Grind a little black pepper on top and add some salt if necessary. Serve immediately, accompanied by the mangetout.

B Increase the amount of potatoes to 350 g (11½ oz) for the 2 servings (this adds 55 calories)

C Increase the amount of potatoes, as for B, and have a corn-on-the-cob as well (this adds 100 calories)

D As for C, and increase the amount of butter to 40 g (2¼ oz) as well (this adds 155 calories)

Salmon fillets with pesto & pasta

CALORIES PER PORTION 510 kCals

A delicious, filling dinner for days when you come home from work feeling starving.

SERVES 2 2 X SALMON FILLETS, WEIGHING ABOUT 125 G (4 OZ) EACH | JUICE OF HALF A LEMON
100 G (3½ OZ) SPAGHETTI (WHOLEMEAL IF POSSIBLE) | 2 TEASPOONS PESTO SAUCE | 1 TEASPOON OLIVE OIL
SALT AND FRESHLY GROUND BLACK PEPPER

1. Preheat the grill to high and put a saucepan of water on to boil.

2. Wipe the salmon fillets clean, run them briefly under the cold tap to rinse, then pat them dry with kitchen paper. Squeeze the lemon juice into a heatproof dish and place the salmon fillets in it. Turn them around in the lemon juice, and leave them skin side up. Place the dish under the hot grill for 5 minutes.

3. Put a pinch of salt in the saucepan of water, and when it is boiling, add the pasta, then leave it to cook.

4. Put the pesto in a small dish, add the olive oil and mix it in well. Take the salmon out from under the grill and turn it skin-side down. Using a small knife, spread a third of the pesto mixture on the top of each fillet. Put back under the grill and cook for a further 5 minutes or until the salmon is cooked right through and the pesto is bubbling and beginning to colour.

5. Just before the salmon is done, the spaghetti should be ready. Drain it, return it to the pan and stir in the rest of the pesto; it will just be enough to give a little added flavour to the pasta. Combine well, over a very low heat, until the pasta is coated.

6. Divide the pasta between 2 plates, and then put a fillet of salmon on top of each one. Season and serve immediately.

B Have a large green salad dressed with ½ tablespoon olive oil and a good splash of balsamic vinegar (this adds 60 calories)

C Increase the amount of spaghetti to 150 g (5 oz) (this adds 90 calories)

D As for C and B combined (this adds 150 calories)

Grilled plaice with a lemon & orange sauce & new potatoes

CALORIES PER PORTION 400 kCals

Use full-fat crème fraîche for this recipe, as the low-fat version might cause the sauce to split.

SERVES 2 250 G (8 OZ) NEW POTATOES | 200 G (7 OZ) PURPLE SPROUTING BROCCOLI, TRIMMED
2 X PLAICE FILLETS, WEIGHING ABOUT 200–250 G (7–8 OZ) EACH | JUICE OF 1 ORANGE
JUICE OF HALF A SMALL LEMON | ½ TEASPOON SUGAR | A FEW THYME LEAVES | 2 TABLESPOONS CRÈME FRAÎCHE
SALT AND FRESHLY GROUND BLACK PEPPER

1. Put the potatoes in a saucepan of lightly salted water and bring to the boil. Put another saucepan of water on to boil for the broccoli. When the potatoes are nearly ready, preheat the grill to high, and put the broccoli into the pan of boiling water.

2. Wipe the plaice fillets clean, run them briefly under the cold tap to rinse, then pat them dry with kitchen paper. Put the plaice on a non-stick baking sheet.

3. Using a small non-stick pan, warm the orange and lemon juice over a medium heat and add the sugar and thyme leaves. Spoon a little of this liquid over the fish and put them under the grill.

4. Put the pan of juices back on the heat, bring up to the boil and reduce the amount of liquid. Check the fish fillets after 2 minutes – they are ready as soon as the flesh is opaque and flakes easily; how long this takes will depend on the size of the fillets. Once they are ready, keep them warm and quickly finish the sauce.

5. Take the pan of sauce off the heat and stir in the crème fraîche. Return it to the heat briefly to warm it up and reduce it slightly, stirring continuously until the sauce has reduced by half, though it will still be quite liquid.

6. Drain the potatoes and broccoli and divide between 2 warmed plates. Put a fillet of fish on each one, and drizzle the citrus sauce around the fish. Season, and serve immediately.

B Increase the amount of potatoes to 400 g (13 oz) between the 2 servings (this adds 55 calories)

C As for B, but have a 10 g (½ oz) sliver of butter on top of each portion of potatoes as well (this adds 130 calories)

D As for B, but divide a 20 g (¾ oz) sliver of butter between the potatoes and the broccoli per portion (this adds 205 calories)

Spicy North African prawns with rice

CALORIES PER PORTION 360 kCals

This dish packs a punch on flavour but is surprisingly quick and easy to prepare.

SERVES 2 100 G (3½ OZ) LONG-GRAIN OR BASMATI RICE | 1 TABLESPOON SUNFLOWER OIL
1 GARLIC CLOVE, FINELY CHOPPED | 1 TEASPOON PAPRIKA | ½ TEASPOON GROUND CUMIN | A PINCH OF GINGER
½ TEASPOON CAYENNE (OR 1 TEASPOON, IF YOU LIKE THE HEAT) | JUICE OF 1 LEMON | 1 TEASPOON CLEAR HONEY
300 G (10 OZ) COOKED PEELED KING PRAWNS
A HANDFUL OF FRESH CORIANDER, LEAVES ONLY, CHOPPED | SALT

1. Get everything ready as you would for a stir-fry before you start cooking, as the prawns cook very quickly. Prepare the rice first. Rinse it and either cook in your usual way, or put 600 ml (1 pint) water in a saucepan and bring it to the boil, then add the rice. Stir it and return to the boil. Cook it, uncovered for about 12–15 minutes, until tender. Take the pan off the heat while you cook the prawns.

2. Put the oil in a frying pan over a medium to high heat, and add the chopped garlic. When you can smell the garlic cooking, stir in the spices. Stir them around briefly, then add the lemon juice, honey and prawns. Cook for a few seconds, still stirring, add almost all the coriander and cook for a further minute. Take the pan off the heat and check the seasoning, adding a little salt if necessary.

3. Drain the rice, rinse it in boiling water, and divide it between 2 plates. Spoon the prawns and their juices over the rice and serve immediately, garnished with the remaining coriander leaves.

B Increase the amount of prawns to 400 g (13 oz) prawns between 2 servings (this adds 50 calories)

C As for B, and also increase the amount of rice to 150 g (5 oz), dry weight, between 2 servings (this adds 140 calories)

D As for B, and also increase the amount of rice to 175 g (6 oz), dry weight, between 2 servings and accompany with a warmed wholemeal pitta bread as well (this adds 330 calories)

Prawn & vegetable stir-fry

CALORIES PER PORTION 400 kCals

Ginger, garlic, soy sauce, chilli and lemon juice: these five basic ingredients will give an oriental flavour to any stir-fry.

SERVES 2 200 G (7 OZ) COOKED PEELED KING PRAWNS | 1 RED PEPPER | 1 SMALL ONION | 1 CARROT
A QUARTER OF A CUCUMBER | 50 G (2 OZ) MUSHROOMS | 1 GARLIC CLOVE
A 2 CM (JUST UNDER 1 INCH) PIECE OF FRESH ROOT GINGER | 1 TABLESPOON SUNFLOWER OR SESAME OIL
1 TEASPOON LIGHT SOY SAUCE | 2 TEASPOONS SWEET CHILLI DIPPING SAUCE
2 TEASPOONS LEMON JUICE, OR TO TASTE | 1 TEASPOON SESAME SEEDS
SERVE WITH: BOILED RICE, MADE WITH 100 G (3½ OZ) DRY RICE

1. Rinse the prawns, pat dry and set to one side. Put the rice on to boil and prepare the vegetables: deseed the pepper and cut it into fine strips, slice the onion into rings and cut the carrot into slender sticks. Cut the cucumber in half and remove the seeds, then cut that into fine strips as well. Trim and slice the mushrooms finely too. Crush the garlic onto a small dish, and then grate the ginger onto it too.

2. Heat the oil in a non-stick wok or very large frying pan. When it is really hot, add the pepper, onion and carrot. Cook them for a couple of minutes, stirring constantly, until they begin to soften. By now the rice should be ready, so drain it and keep it warm.

3. Add the cucumber and mushrooms, garlic and ginger to the wok. Stir for a minute or so more, add the soy sauce and stir, then add the prawns. Stir-fry for a further 2 minutes then add the chilli sauce and lemon juice, and allow those to simmer briefly. Sprinkle in the sesame seeds, stir everything around once more and then serve immediately, accompanied by the boiled rice.

B Increase the amount of rice to 150 g (5 oz) between the 2 servings (this adds 90 calories)

C As for B, and increase the amount of prawns to 300 g (10 oz) between the 2 servings as well (this adds 140 calories)

D As for C, but add 10 g (½oz) cashew nuts with the prawns (this adds 200 calories)

Pasta with creamy chicken

CALORIES PER PORTION without the Parmesan: 590 kCals; with the Parmesan: 630 kCals

This is a handy way to use up leftover chicken, making a tasty meal that all the family will enjoy.

SERVES 2 2 TEASPOONS OLIVE OIL | 1 LARGE ONION, FINELY CHOPPED | 1 GARLIC CLOVE, FINELY CHOPPED
175 G (6 OZ) WHOLEMEAL PASTA (PENNE OR RIGATONI)
125 G (4 OZ) COLD COOKED CHICKEN BREAST, SKIN REMOVED, CUT INTO STRIPS (FOR RECIPE, SEE PAGE 58)
6 MUSHROOMS, CLEANED AND SLICED (INCLUDE STALKS, IF GOOD) | A SMALL THYME SPRIG, LEAVES ONLY
100 G (3½ OZ) LOW-FAT CRÈME FRAÎCHE | 1 TEASPOON FRENCH MUSTARD
20 G (¾ OZ) GRATED PARMESAN (OPTIONAL) | SALT AND FRESHLY GROUND BLACK PEPPER

SERVE WITH: SALAD LEAVES

1. Heat the oil in a large frying pan over a medium heat. Add the onion and fry gently for about 5 minutes until it is softened but not brown. Then add the garlic and cook for a further minute.

2. Bring a large saucepan of water to the boil and add the pasta and a pinch of salt.

3. Put the chopped chicken in the frying pan with the onions and stir well. Allow it to cook for a couple of minutes, but add a little water if the onions seem to be burning – stir as it cooks, and it should be fine without.

4. Add the mushrooms to the pan and continue cooking – the mushrooms will soon begin to release their juices. Add the thyme leaves, raise the heat slightly and cook the juices off – this should take a couple of minutes. Lower the heat and add the crème fraîche and mustard, a little salt and lots of black pepper, and cook gently for a further couple of minutes.

5. By now the pasta should be ready. Drain it, and divide between 2 warmed serving dishes or bowls. Spoon the creamy chicken over the pasta, sprinkle some grated Parmesan on top and serve immediately, accompanied by a green salad.

B Add a dressing to the salad (2 teaspoons olive oil and 1 teaspoon lemon juice) as well (this adds 90 calories)

C As for B, and increase the amount of pasta to 200 g (7 oz) between the 2 servings (this adds 135 calories)

D As for C, but increase the amount of cooked chicken to 200 g (7 oz) between the 2 servings as well (this adds 195 calories)

Stir-fried chicken with mangetout or green beans

CALORIES PER PORTION 425 kCals

Substitute any leftover vegetables in this tasty stir-fry: baby corn, asparagus, pak choi, sliced courgette – whatever you have in the fridge.

SERVES 2 2 X SKINLESS CHICKEN BREASTS, WEIGHING ABOUT 100 G (3½ OZ) EACH | JUICE OF A LEMON
1 TEASPOON LIGHT SOY SAUCE | 2 TEASPOONS CLEAR HONEY | 100 G (3½ OZ) MANGETOUT OR GREEN BEANS, TRIMMED
50 G (2 OZ) PURPLE SPROUTING BROCCOLI | 10 SPRING ONIONS | 1 LARGE RED PEPPER, DESEEDED
2 GARLIC CLOVES | 1 SMALL GREEN CHILLI, DESEEDED (OPTIONAL) | 1 TABLESPOON SUNFLOWER OR SESAME OIL
SERVE WITH: 100 G (3½ OZ) LONG-GRAIN RICE (DRY WEIGHT)

1. Cut the chicken into strips not larger than 3 x 1 cm (1¼ x ½ inch). Put them in a bowl and add half the lemon juice, the soy sauce and the honey. Stir them to coat, cover the bowl and put it in the fridge for 30 minutes.

2. Put the rice on to boil and prepare the vegetables. Cut the mangetout or beans into pieces no longer than 3 cm (1¼ inch), remove the lower parts of the stems of the sprouting broccoli, and cut the spring onions diagonally – include some of the green part. Slice the pepper into fine strips. Finely chop the garlic and the green chilli (if using).

3. Use a non-stick wok or a very large non-stick frying pan. Put it over a high heat, add the oil and take the chicken out of the fridge. Using a slotted spoon, remove the chicken from the marinade and add it to the wok. Cook for about 3–4 minutes, stirring well until it begins to colour, then remove it from the wok and set aside.

4. Add the chopped vegetables, garlic and chilli and cook them quickly until they are crisp but tender; keep stirring or they will catch and burn. Keep an eye on the rice as the stir-fry cooks, and remove it from the heat as soon as it is ready. Return the chicken to the wok, add the rest of the lemon juice and allow the chicken to warm up thoroughly – about another minute. Drain the rice and serve it immediately, with the stir-fry.

B Use larger chicken breasts, about 150 g (5 oz) each (this adds 60 calories)

C Increase the amount of rice to 150 g (5 oz), dry weight, between the 2 servings (this adds 90 calories)

D As for B and increase the amount of rice to 175 g (6 oz), dry weight, between the 2 servings (this adds 195 calories)

Chicken with olives, lemon & chickpeas

CALORIES PER PORTION 465 kCals

The succulent chicken, meaty chickpeas and Middle Eastern flavours make this dish a Biggest Loser favourite.

SERVES 2 2 LARGE SKINLESS CHICKEN BREASTS, WEIGHING ABOUT 175 G (6 OZ) EACH | 2 TEASPOONS OLIVE OIL
1 ONION, FINELY CHOPPED | 2 GARLIC CLOVES, FINELY CHOPPED
1 TEASPOON PAPRIKA (SWEET PAPRIKA IF POSSIBLE) | A SMALL PINCH OF TURMERIC
400–500 ML (14–17 FL OZ) WATER, OR A HALF-AND-HALF MIXTURE OF WATER AND CHICKEN STOCK
JUICE OF 1 LARGE LEMON | 1 X 400G TIN OF CHICKPEAS, DRAINED AND RINSED | 20 BLACK OLIVES IN BRINE, PITTED
A MINT SPRIG, PLUS A FEW LEAVES | SALT AND FRESHLY GROUND BLACK PEPPER

SERVE WITH: SALAD LEAVES

1. Cut each chicken breast into 4–5 pieces. Put the oil in a large saucepan with a lid and warm it over a medium heat. Add the onion and cook for 5 minutes or until it is softened but not brown. Then add the garlic, paprika and turmeric and stir them into the onions. Put the chicken pieces into the pan, and stir well to coat them with the spicy mixture.

2. Add the water (or stock and water) to cover and the lemon juice. Bring to the boil and then reduce the heat and simmer gently with the pan covered. Cook for 15 minutes, keeping an eye on the pan and adding more liquid if necessary.

3. Then add the chickpeas. Cover the pan again, and continue to cook and monitor the level of liquid for another 10 minutes.

4. Drain and rinse the olives then cut them in half. Add the olives and the mint sprig to the pan, and cook for a further 5 minutes. Check the seasoning, and check that the chicken is cooked.

5. Remove what is left of the sprig of mint, then lift the chicken pieces out with a slotted spoon and keep them warm. The liquid should be much reduced and quite thick, but if there is still a lot of liquid in the pan, raise the heat and boil rapidly, stirring, until there is much less.

6. Divide the chickpeas between 2 plates, place the chicken pieces on top and garnish with the mint leaves. Serve immediately, accompanied by a green salad.

B Add a dressing to the salad (2teaspoons olive oil and 1 teaspoon balsamic vinegar) (this adds 90 calories)

C As for B, and have half a wholemeal roll with 1 teaspoon low-fat spread as well (this adds 230 calories)

D As for B, and have an entire wholemeal roll with 2 teaspoons low-fat spread as well (this adds 370 calories)

Marinated chicken kebabs

CALORIES PER PORTION 465 kCals

You'll need skewers to thread the chicken onto: your supermarket should have either wooden, bamboo or metal ones. They'll also come in handy for the fruit kebabs on page 163.

SERVES 2 2 SKINLESS CHICKEN BREASTS, WEIGHING ABOUT 175 G (6 OZ) EACH | 1 ONION | 2 GARLIC CLOVES, CRUSHED
1 TABLESPOON OLIVE OIL | JUICE OF 1 LEMON | FRESHLY GROUND BLACK PEPPER
1 STANDARD-SIZE WHOLEMEAL PITTA BREAD | 200 G (7 OZ) LOW-FAT GREEK YOGURT
A QUARTER OF A CUCUMBER |

SERVE WITH: SALAD LEAVES

1. Rinse and pat dry the chicken breasts with kitchen paper.

2. If you have a food processor or blender, chop the onion and put it in the processor with the garlic, olive oil, lemon juice and some black pepper, then whizz them together until you have a paste. If you haven't, grate the onion and garlic into a bowl, add the oil, lemon juice and pepper and mix everything together well.

3. Cut the chicken breasts into 2 cm (just under 1 inch) pieces and put them in a bowl. Spoon the onion mixture over them and rub it in well, ensuring that all the pieces have been coated with the mix. Cover the bowl and put it in the fridge for at least 2 hours.

4. If you are using bamboo or wooden skewers, soak them in water for 30 minutes before you need them. Preheat the grill to a medium to high heat, and thread the chicken pieces onto the skewers. Find a roasting dish big enough for the ends of the skewers to rest on the sides, suspending the chicken and allowing it to cook properly, then place it under the hot grill.

5. Grill the kebabs for 5 minutes, then turn the skewers over and cook for another 5–10 minutes, or until the chicken is done.

6. Towards the end of cooking, put the pitta breads under the grill to warm. Put the yogurt in a bowl; finely chop the cucumber and stir it into the yogurt with a lot of black pepper.

7. Arrange the skewers on a plate and put some of the cucumber and yogurt alongside. Serve immediately, with the warm pitta bread and a green salad.

B Add a dressing to the salad (2 teaspoons olive oil and 1 teaspoon lemon juice) as well (this adds 90 calories)

C As for B, and increase the amount of yogurt to 300 g (10 oz) between the two servings (this adds 130 calories)

D As for C, but have a whole pitta bread per serving as well (this adds 205 calories)

Chicken curry with yogurt (and a kick)

CALORIES PER PORTION 420–450 kCals, depending on the size of the chicken breasts, including the rice

Curries served in Indian restaurants tend to be chock-full of calories and fat but this healthy, low-cal version tastes every bit as good. Vary the amount of chilli to taste.

SERVES 4 4 LARGE SKINLESS CHICKEN BREASTS, WEIGHING ABOUT 150–175 G (6 OZ) EACH
1 TEASPOON GROUND CORIANDER | 1 TEASPOON GROUND CUMIN | ½ TEASPOON TURMERIC
½ TEASPOON GROUND GINGER | ½–1 TEASPOON CHILLI POWDER (OR TO TASTE)
1 TABLESPOON RAPESEED OR SUNFLOWER OIL | 1 LARGE ONION, FINELY CHOPPED | 2 GARLIC CLOVES, FINELY CHOPPED
200 ML (7 FL OZ) WATER | 1 TEASPOON TOMATO PURÉE | 1 TEASPOON PLAIN FLOUR | 150 G (5 OZ) NATURAL YOGURT
FRESH CORIANDER, LEAVES ONLY, FINELY CHOPPED, TO GARNISH

SERVE WITH: PLAIN BOILED RICE, 200 G (7 OZ) DRY WEIGHT, PREFERABLY BASMATI

1. Rinse the chicken breasts and pat them dry with kitchen paper. Cut them into cubes no bigger than 2 cm (just under 1 inch). Mix all the spices together in a small bowl.

2. Put the oil in a large saucepan over a medium to high heat and add the onion. Stir continuously for about 10 minutes, until it starts to brown. Add the spices, stir well and cook gently until the scent of roasting spices rises. Put the chicken pieces in the pan too, and stir them around for another minute. Add the water and tomato purée and cook for 5 minutes.

3. Combine the flour with a little water, blending it well, then add it to the yogurt and mix it in well (this will help to stabilize the yogurt and stop it separating in cooking). Lower the heat and add the yogurt to the curry.

4. Cover and cook gently for 1–1¼ hours, checking every 20 minutes or so that nothing is catching (add a little water if necessary). Towards the end of this period, put the rice on to boil.

5. This is not a dry curry and should be fairly liquid, but increase the heat slightly to reduce the liquid a little more if you wish – and serve with the plain boiled rice when it is cooked. Scatter with the coriander.

B B Increase the amount of rice to 300 g (10 oz) between the 2 servings (this adds 90 calories)

C As for B, and have 1 plain ready-to-cook poppadum, cooked in the microwave (allow 1 minute) as well (this adds 120 calories)

D As for B, and have a standard wholemeal pitta bread, warmed in the oven, per serving (this adds 240 calories)

Lamb curry with coconut milk

CALORIES PER PORTION for the curry: 555 kCals; for the rice: 135 kCals

Be sure to buy light coconut milk for this Thai-style curry, as it's got far fewer calories than the full-fat type.

SERVES 4 2 TEASPOONS VEGETABLE OIL | 1 LARGE ONION, CHOPPED | 2 GARLIC CLOVES, FINELY CHOPPED
1 KG (2 LB) DICED LAMB | 1 TEASPOONS GROUND CORIANDER | 1 TEASPOONS GARAM MASALA
½ TEASPOONS TURMERIC | 2–3 GREEN CHILLIES (OR TO TASTE), DESEEDED AND FINELY CHOPPED
1 X 400 ML (14 FL OZ) CAN OF LIGHT COCONUT MILK | 1 TEASPOON PLAIN FLOUR
2 TOMATOES, SKINNED AND CHOPPED | SALT
SERVE WITH: BOILED BASMATI RICE, 160 G (5½ OZ), DRY WEIGHT

1. Put the oil in a large non-stick saucepan or heatproof casserole with a lid and warm it over a gentle heat. Add the onion and cook gently for 10 minutes, then add the garlic and continue cooking until the onion has softened and is beginning to colour.

2. Add the cubes of lamb and brown them until they are sealed on all sides. Remove them from the pan with a slotted spoon and set to one side.

3. Add the coriander, garam masala and turmeric to the pan and stir them together for a minute, then add the chillies and stir again.

4. In a jug or bowl, whisk the coconut milk and flour really well, making sure there are no lumps remaining. Add the coconut milk to the pan and stir, then add the chopped tomato. When the liquid begins to simmer, return the lamb to the pan.

5. Cover the pan and cook the lamb gently until tender, adding some boiling water if necessary to stop it catching. How long it will take depends the size of the pieces, but could be from 45–55 minutes – test it to see. When the curry is almost ready, rinse the rice and put it in a pan of hot water. Bring to the boil and cook until the rice is tender.

6. This should be a relatively dry curry, so if there is still quite a bit of liquid left, turn up the heat so that it boils off. Check for tenderness and seasoning, adding a little salt if necessary, and remove the pan from the heat. Drain and rinse the cooked rice with boiling water, and serve the curry immediately.

B Have a green salad, dressed with 1 teaspoon sunflower oil and a squeeze of lemon juice as well (this adds 50 calories)

C As for B, and increase the amount of rice to 200 g (7 oz), dry weight, between the 4 servings (this adds 85 calories)

D As for C, and have half a standard wholemeal pitta bread each (or a chapatti, see page 98) as well (this adds 160 calories)

Lamb cutlet with chickpeas, shallots & parsley

CALORIES PER PORTION 480 kCals

A dish that's so rich and flavourful, you'll never believe it is part of a
weight-loss programme..

SERVES 2 2 LAMB CUTLETS OR LARGE CHOPS, WEIGHING ABOUT 100 G (3½ OZ) EACH | JUICE OF 1 SMALL LEMON
2 TEASPOONS OLIVE OIL | 1 GARLIC CLOVE, CRUSHED | 1 X 400 G (13 OZ) CAN OF CHICKPEAS, DRAINED AND RINSED
2 ROSEMARY SPRIGS (OPTIONAL) | 2 LARGE SHALLOTS, FINELY CHOPPED
A HANDFUL OF FLAT-LEAF PARSLEY, FINELY CHOPPED

SERVE WITH: 200 G (7 OZ) GREEN BEANS

1. Trim the excess fat off the cutlets or chops, especially along the bone, but try not to remove any meat as well. In a small bowl, whisk together the lemon juice, olive oil and garlic. Put the chops on a plate and drizzle a teaspoon of the liquid over each chop.

2. Preheat the grill to high. Put the chickpeas in a saucepan. Cover with fresh water and put the pan over a medium to high heat. Bring to the boil, then reduce the heat and simmer for 3 minutes – they should be hot but not disintegrating. In a separate pan, boil the green beans until tender.

3. Put some aluminium foil on the grill pan, add a couple of sprigs of rosemary and place a chop on top of each one. Spoon a little of the lemon liquid over each chop. Grill for 3–5 minutes on each side (keeping the rosemary beneath them when you turn them over), depending on how thick the chops are and how well done you want them to be.

4. Meanwhile, drain the chickpeas when they are done and put them in a bowl. Add the shallots and parsley, and pour over the remaining lemon liquid. Stir well, and set aside until the lamb is ready.

5. Put half the chickpeas on each plate, and serve with the lamb on top and the green beans alongside.

B Have a side salad of mixed leaves dressed with 2 teaspoons olive oil and 1 teaspoon lemon juice as well (this adds 90 calories)

C As for B, and have a large slice of wholemeal bread to mop up the juices per serving as well (this adds 190 calories)

D Have 2 lamb chops per serving – still trimming the fat well before cooking (this adds 250 calories)

Moroccan lamb casserole with apricots

CALORIES PER PORTION 635 kCals

With the sweetness of apricots and the warmth of spices, this dish tastes like an expensive gourmet creation, but in fact it couldn't be simpler to make.

SERVES 2 1 TEASPOON OLIVE OIL | 1 ONION, FINELY CHOPPED | ½ TEASPOON CINNAMON
¼ TEASPOON GROUND CUMIN | A PINCH OF CHILLI POWDER OR PAPRIKA, TO TASTE
400 G (13 OZ) DICED LAMB OR LAMB LEG STEAKS, CHOPPED | 1 FAT GARLIC CLOVE, FINELY CHOPPED
ABOUT 250–350 ML (8–12 FL OZ) WATER | 1 TABLESPOON TOMATO PURÉE | SALT AND FRESHLY GROUND BLACK PEPPER
125 G (4 OZ) DRIED APRICOTS | 75 G (3 OZ) COUSCOUS | 100 ML (3½ FL OZ) BOILING WATER

SERVE WITH: SALAD LEAVES

1. Warm the oil in a heavy-based saucepan or heatproof casserole with a lid, and add the chopped onion. Cook over a gentle heat for about 5 minutes, until it is just beginning to colour. Add the cinnamon, cumin and chilli powder or paprika and stir. Then add the lamb and stir it in, ensuring that all the pieces are coated in the spices. Add the garlic, stir it around, and then add enough water to cover (probably about 250 ml/8 fl oz), the tomato purée and lots of black pepper.

2. Gently simmer the stew, covered, for about 1½ hours – by which time the lamb should be tender. Check on it every so often and top it up with more water if the level gets very low. Then add the apricots and cook, gently, for a further 30 minutes. Be careful that it doesn't catch and start to burn at this stage – check regularly, stir, and add some more liquid if necessary.

3. When the stew is nearly ready, prepare the couscous. Put it in a large bowl and add the boiling water. Stir well, cover and set aside for 5 minutes. By the end of this time the couscous should be soft – if not, leave it a little longer. It should also have absorbed all the water, but if it hasn't, drain it with a sieve. Put it back in the bowl and fluff it up with a fork, breaking up any lumps.

4. Serve the stew with the couscous and a green salad.

B Increase the amount of couscous to 120 g (4 oz) (this adds 70 calories)

C As for B, and increase the amount of lamb to 500 g (1 lb) as well (this adds 160 calories)

D Increase the amount of lamb to 500 g (1 lb) and the amount of couscous to 150 g (5 oz) (this adds 215 calories)

Pork fillet with lentils & mustard

CALORIES PER PORTION 500 kCals

Don't worry if you've never cooked lentils: it couldn't be easier! They're a great source of protein, fibre and vitamin B1.

SERVES 2 100 G (3½ OZ) SMALL LENTILS (PUY LENTILS IF POSSIBLE) | 300 G (10 OZ) PORK FILLET
2 TEASPOONS OLIVE OIL | 1 RED ONION, FINELY CHOPPED | 1 THYME SPRIG, LEAVES ONLY
2 TEASPOONS WHOLEGRAIN MUSTARD | 600 ML (1 PINT) HOT WATER OR VEGETABLE STOCK
6 SUN-DRIED TOMATOES IN OIL | SALT AND FRESHLY GROUND BLACK PEPPER

SERVE WITH: 200 G (7 OZ) BROCCOLI

1. Put the lentils in a saucepan, cover with water and bring to the boil. Cook for about 2 minutes, skimming off any scum that forms, then drain and rinse them.

2. Rinse and pat dry the pork fillet with kitchen paper, and cut it into rounds about 5 mm (¼ inch) thick – there should be enough for about 10 rounds.

3. Heat the oil in a large non-stick frying pan (one which has a lid or can be covered), and add the medallions of pork – the oil may spit, so be careful. Sear them quickly on one side, then flip them over and brown the other side slightly. Remove and set aside.

4. Add the onion to the pan and cook for a couple of minutes, then add the drained lentils and the thyme. Stir the mustard into the water or stock and pour it into the pan. Cook, more gently, for 10 minutes and check that nothing is sticking; stir regularly.

5. Rinse the sun-dried tomatoes and pat them dry, then cut them into chunks and add them to the lentil pan. Cook for a further 5 minutes, then lay the slices of pork fillet on top of the lentils, cover the pan and cook gently for 5 more minutes.

6. Boil the broccoli until tender. Meanwhile, put another, smaller, non-stick frying pan on the hob over a high heat. Take the lid off the larger pan, remove the slices of fillet and put them in the smaller pan – it should not be necessary to add any oil. Brown one side for about 2 minutes, then flip them over and brown the other; at the same time, increase the heat under the lentils to reduce the amount of liquid, if necessary.

7. Check the lentils are soft, then divide them between 2 plates. Put the medallions of pork on top of the lentils and serve immediately with the broccoli.

B Have a green salad a chopped tomato, dressed with 1 teaspoon olive oil and drizzled with a little lemon juice as well
(this adds 70 calories)

C Have 150 g (5 oz) new potatoes as well – boil and drain them and then put them back in the pan and add 1 teaspoon wholegrain mustard; stir together and serve with the rest of the dish
(this adds 120 calories)

D As for B and C combined
(this adds 190 calories)

Chilli con carne

CALORIES PER PORTION 500 kCals

Buy mince that is marked 'extra lean'. It's got far fewer calories than full-fat mince and is much healthier for your heart.

SERVES 4 2 TEASPOONS OLIVE OIL | 2 ONIONS, FINELY CHOPPED | 2 GARLIC CLOVES, CRUSHED
1 TEASPOON GROUND CUMIN | 2 TEASPOONS MIXED DRIED HERBS | 2 BAY LEAVES
750 G (1½ LB) EXTRA LEAN MINCED BEEF | 1 TEASPOON PAPRIKA | ½ TEASPOON CAYENNE PEPPER (OR TO TASTE)
2 TABLESPOONS TOMATO PURÉE | 1 X 400 G (13 OZ) CAN CHOPPED TOMATOES | 100 ML (3½ FL OZ) RED WINE
200 ML (7 FL OZ) WATER | 1 X 400 G (13 OZ) CAN KIDNEY BEANS | SALT AND FRESHLY GROUND BLACK PEPPER

SERVE WITH: SALAD LEAVES

1. Warm the oil in a large heavy-based saucepan or heatproof casserole. Gently fry the onions for about 5–10 minutes until softened, but not brown. Stir in the garlic, cumin, mixed herbs and bay leaves. Cook for a minute then add the minced beef. Brown the meat, stirring and breaking up any lumps.

2. Add the paprika, cayenne pepper and tomato purée and stir everything thoroughly. Add the chopped tomatoes, and pour in the wine and water. Put a lid on the pan or casserole and cook over a very low heat for 1 ½ hours; every 20–30 minutes give the chilli a stir and check that it isn't catching on the base of the pan, adding a little more water if necessary.

3. Drain and rinse the kidney beans, then add them to the meat and cook for a further 30 minutes. Check the seasoning, remove the bay leaves and serve immediately, accompanied by a green salad.

B Have a small baked potato, about 150 g (5 oz) per serving as well (this adds 115 calories)

C Have some boiled rice (about 50 g/2 oz dry weight) and 10 g (½ oz) grated Cheddar cheese on top of the chilli per serving (this adds 210 calories)

D Have some boiled rice (about 75 g/3 oz) with the chilli and 20 g (¾ oz grated Cheddar cheese per serving as well (this adds 340 calories)

Steak with herby, healthy chips

CALORIES PER PORTION 440 kCals

This is a good example of a traditional meal that's been adapted to have a lower calorie count, but with extra flavour.

SERVES 2 2 X FILLET STEAKS, WEIGHING ABOUT 150 G (5 OZ) EACH | 50 ML (2 FL OZ) RED WINE
2 TEASPOONS OLIVE OIL | FRESHLY GROUND BLACK PEPPER | MUSTARD, TO SERVE

FOR THE CHIPS: 2 BAKING POTATOES, WEIGHING ABOUT 175 G (6 OZ) EACH | 2 TEASPOONS OLIVE OIL
1 TEASPOON DRIED MIXED HERBS

1. Trim any excess fat from the steaks. Pour the wine into a china dish, add a good grinding of black pepper then turn the steaks over in this marinade so they are evenly coated. Cover the dish and set aside until needed.

2. After 30 minutes, prepare the chips. Preheat the oven to 200°C (400°F) Gas mark 6. Wash the potatoes but don't peel them. Slice them into fat chips (about 2 cm/just under 1 inch wide). Place them in a pan of water, bring to the boil and par-boil for 2 minutes.

3. Drizzle the oil into a large ovenproof dish and place it in the preheated oven to warm.

Drain the potatoes and put them in the warm oil, then sprinkle the herbs on top. Turn well to coat, and spread them out in a single layer. Put the dish back in the oven and bake for 10–12 minutes. Remove the dish, turn the chips over, moving them around, and return to the oven for a further 10–15 minutes until they are browning nicely.

4. When the chips are almost ready, heat the olive oil in a large frying pan or ridged griddle pan. When the oil is starting to smoke, take the steaks out of their marinade and cook them to taste, turning once. Serve immediately, with the herby chips and a little mustard.

B Have a mixed leaf salad with 4 cherry tomatoes and 1 tablespoon of ready-made light vinaigrette dressing as well (this adds 75 calories)

C As for B, and also have a larger steak, weighing up to 225 g (7½ oz) each as well (this adds 180 calories)

D As for B and C combined, plus a 125 ml (4 fl oz) glass of red wine to accompany it (this adds 275 calories)

Desserts

Strawberry ice

CALORIES PER PORTION 95 kCals

Ice cream is usually high in calories because of the sugar and cream it contains, but this sorbet is calorie-light and has an intense strawberry flavour.

SERVES 4 250 G (8 OZ) RIPE STRAWBERRIES, HULLED AND CHOPPED | 75 G (3 OZ) CASTER SUGAR
300 ML (½ PINT) WATER | 4 MINT SPRIGS, LEAVES ONLY, TO SERVE

1. Put the strawberries in a saucepan with the sugar and water. Cook them gently over a medium heat until the sugar has dissolved and the strawberries have broken up.

2. Balance a sieve over a large bowl and gradually pour the strawberry liquid through; help the process by gently pushing with a wooden spoon but don't push too hard – you want to end up with juice, not a fruit purée. Allow the liquid to cool, and keep the sieve over the bowl so it can continue dripping.

3. Once the juice is cold, pour it into a sealable freezer-proof container. Transfer it to the freezer for about an hour, then remove the container and stir the partly frozen contents thoroughly using a fork, drawing the already-frozen edges into the middle and breaking up the ice crystals. Freeze for a further 2 hours and repeat, then freeze for a little longer if it seems necessary; you will end up with flakes of bright red strawberry ice with an intense flavour.

4. Take the container out of the freezer about 10 minutes before serving to allow the strawberry ice to soften sufficiently, then use a fork to break up the larger crystals. Spoon it into 4 serving dishes – wine glasses look great – and serve immediately with sprig of mint on top of each. Any unused ice can be returned to the freezer.

Golden fruit salad with cinnamon & vanilla

CALORIES PER PORTION 155 kCals

With a glorious colour as well as a rich flavour, we highly recommend this fabulous fruit salad.

SERVES 2 2 ORANGES, 1 JUICED AND THE OTHER PEELED, PIPPED AND CUT INTO SEGMENTS | JUICE OF HALF A LEMON
A PINCH OF CINNAMON | A SPLASH OF ORANGE-FLOWER WATER (OPTIONAL)
2 TEASPOONS VANILLA SUGAR (OR 2 TEASPOONS SUGAR PLUS A COUPLE OF DROPS OF VANILLA ESSENCE)
HALF A CANTALOUPE MELON, CUT INTO CHUNKS NO BIGGER THAN 2 CM (JUST UNDER 1 INCH)
2 LARGE VICTORIA PLUMS, CHOPPED | 1 PEACH OR NECTARINE, CHOPPED

1. Mix the orange and lemon juice together in a bowl, add the cinnamon and orange-flower water, if using, and then stir in the sugar. Whisk until the sugar has dissolved.

2. Put all the fruit into a mixing bowl, then pour the spiced liquid over it and stir gently. Cover and refrigerate for at least 2 hours before serving.

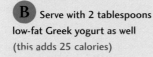 **B** Serve with 2 tablespoons low-fat Greek yogurt as well (this adds 25 calories)

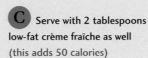 **C** Serve with 2 tablespoons low-fat crème fraîche as well (this adds 50 calories)

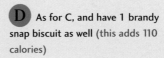 **D** As for C, and have 1 brandy snap biscuit as well (this adds 110 calories)

Scottish cream

CALORIES PER PORTION 230 kCals

If you don't like whisky, this would also work with dark rum or brandy – or you could make it without booze and knock 22 calories off the total.

SERVES 2 10 G (½ OZ) ALMONDS | 45 G (1½ OZ) JUMBO OATS | 2 TABLESPOONS LOW-FAT GREEK YOGURT
4 TABLESPOONS LOW-FAT CRÈME FRAÎCHE | 2 TEASPOONS CLEAR HONEY | 2 TEASPOONS WHISKY (OPTIONAL)

1. Preheat the grill to high. Chop the almonds finely. Don't whizz them in a food processor or blender as they could become powdery, but you could try putting them in a sealable plastic bag, sealing the bag, and then hitting them with a rolling pin. Once chopped, spread them out on a baking sheet, add the oats and then place the sheet under the hot grill so that they toast. After a couple of minutes, shake the baking sheet and return it to the grill. Keep an eye on the oats and nuts, and take the tray out as soon as they begin to colour; they should not burn. Set them to one side to cool.

2. Put the yogurt and crème fraîche in a bowl and add the honey and whisky, if using; mix them together well. Stir in the toasted oats and almonds.

3. Divide the mixture between 2 serving dishes (ramekins or wine glasses look good), cover with clingfilm and chill in the fridge for at least 2 hours before serving.

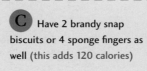 **B** Have a brandy snap biscuit or 2 sponge fingers as well (this adds 60 calories)

C Have 2 brandy snap biscuits or 4 sponge fingers as well (this adds 120 calories)

D As for C, and also chop another 10 g (½ oz) almonds and scatter them over the top of each dish, and drizzle 1 teaspoon honey over each one too (this adds 180 calories)

Orange with toasted pine nuts, honey & yogurt

CALORIES PER PORTION 145 kCals

If you don't have any pine nuts, use almonds instead. Chop three almonds into little pieces and toast them as described.

SERVES 1 | 1 LARGE ORANGE | 1 TEASPOON PINE NUTS | 1 HEAPED TABLESPOON LOW-FAT GREEK YOGURT
1 TEASPOON CLEAR HONEY

1. Preheat the grill to high. Over a plate, peel the orange and remove as much of the white pith as possible. Cut the orange flesh into slices, lay them in a heatproof dish and pour over any juice collected on the plate. Place the dish under the hot grill for the oranges to warm through.

2. Put a dry frying pan over a high heat and add the pine nuts. Use a wooden spoon to move them about and make sure they don't burn; as soon as they begin to change colour and smell toasted, take the pan off the heat.

3. Put the warm orange slices in a serving dish, add the yogurt, scatter the toasted pine nuts over it, and drizzle the honey on top. Serve immediately.

B C D Allow yourself another teaspoon of pine nuts or 3 more almonds (this adds 35 calories) and also double the quantity of yogurt (this adds 25 calories)

Dried apricot fool

CALORIES PER PORTION 255 kCals

You'll feel naughty eating this intensely rich dessert. It doesn't look or taste as though it should be on a weight-loss programme – and yet it is.

SERVES 2 12 DRIED APRICOTS, FINELY CHOPPED | JUICE OF 1 ORANGE | 75 G (3 OZ) LOW-FAT GREEK YOGURT
2 TABLESPOONS LOW-FAT CRÈME FRAÎCHE

1. Put the apricots in a small non-stick pan with the orange juice. Warm them over a medium heat, stirring, until the juice bubbles and the apricots start to soften. Continue stirring until the juice has been absorbed, remove the pan from the heat and empty the apricots into a bowl. Mash them up a little with a fork, then leave to cool.

2. Once the apricots are cool, add the yogurt and crème fraîche to the bowl and stir everything together well. Spoon the mixture into two ramekin dishes or small glasses, cover with clingfilm and put in the fridge to chill for at least 2 hours before serving.

B If you have a sweet tooth, add 1 teaspoon clear honey to the top of each serving (this adds 25 calories)

C Have a brandy snap biscuit as well (this adds 60 calories)

D Have 2 brandy snap biscuits as well (this adds 120 calories)

Nectarines in wine

CALORIES PER PORTION 165 kCals

A light, fragrant pudding for those long summer evenings. And the bonus is that the wine it contains doesn't count as part of your treats allowance!

SERVES 2 3 LARGE NECTARINES OR PEACHES | 175 ML (6 FL OZ) ROSÉ WINE
A 2 CM (JUST UNDER 1 INCH) PIECE OF CINNAMON STICK | 3 CLOVES | 1 TABLESPOON CASTER SUGAR

1. Cut the nectarines in half and twist to remove one half from the stone. Cut or pull the stone from the remaining half. Slice each half into 3 segments.

2. Put the wine, cinnamon, cloves and sugar in a saucepan and warm it over a medium heat until the sugar has dissolved. Add the slices of fruit and raise the temperature until the wine begins to boil. Cook for about 1 minute, or until the

nectarine skins show the first signs of separating from the fruit.

3. Remove the nectarine slices from the wine using a slotted spoon, and put them in 2 serving dishes. Continue boiling the liquid, stirring, until it has reduced by about half – this will probably take a further minute or two. Remove the piece of cinnamon and the cloves, and spoon the spiced wine over the nectarines. Serve immediately.

B Have 1 heaped tablespoon of low-fat Greek yogurt with the nectarines as well (this adds 25 calories)

C Have a brandy snap biscuit as well (this adds 60 calories)

D As for B and C combined (this adds 85 calories).

Fruit kebabs

CALORIES PER PORTION 230 kCals

All the desserts in this book are good … but if the team were voting for their favourite, it would have to be this one!

SERVES 2 1 SMALL TO MEDIUM BANANA | 1 NECTARINE | 4 SMALL READY-TO-EAT STONED PRUNES OR DRIED APRICOTS
JUICE OF HALF A LEMON | 1 TABLESPOON CLEAR HONEY | 50 ML (2 FL OZ) WATER
100 G (3½ OZ) GOOD-QUALITY VANILLA ICE CREAM

1. Soak 2 bamboo skewers in water for 30 minutes (or use metal skewers). Preheat the oven to 220°C (425°F) Gas mark 7.

2. Peel the banana and cut it into 8 pieces. Cut the nectarine into pieces roughly the same size. Thread a prune or apricot onto one of the skewers and push it to the end, then fill up the skewer, alternating banana and nectarine along it, and ending up with another prune or apricot. Fill the second skewer in the same way and then put them both on a baking sheet and sprinkle with the lemon juice.

3. Put the honey in a small non-stick pan and add the water. Bring to the boil, stirring constantly for about 4 minutes, by which time the honey and water will have reduced to a syrup. Drizzle this over the kebabs, then put the dish in the preheated oven. Bake for 3 minutes, then turn the kebabs and cook for another 3 minutes.

4. Remove from the oven, and use a fork to slide the fruit off each kebab into a serving dish. Carefully spoon what is left of the syrup over them (caution: this is very hot). Allow the kebabs to cool slightly, and then add the ice cream. Serve immediately.

B Increase the amount of ice cream to 150 g (5 oz) between the 2 servings (this adds 50 calories)

C Increase the amount of ice cream to 200 g (7 oz) between the 2 servings (this adds 100 calories)

D As for C, and have a fan wafer biscuit each as well (this adds 145 calories)

Vanilla rhubarb with honey & ice cream

CALORIES PER PORTION 200 kCals

Serve the rhubarb hot or cold, as you prefer, but the hot version melts the ice cream making a lovely gooey mess.

SERVES 2 125 G (4 OZ) RHUBARB, TRIMMED AND CHOPPED | 3 TEASPOONS CLEAR HONEY
A FEW DROPS OF VANILLA ESSENCE | 125 ML (4 FL OZ) WATER | 150 G (5 OZ) GOOD-QUALITY VANILLA ICE CREAM

1. Put the rhubarb in a non-stick saucepan and add the honey, vanilla essence and water. Bring to the boil, then reduce the heat and cook for 5 minutes or until the pieces of rhubarb start to fall apart. Mix to make a puree.

2. Remove the pan from the heat, pour the rhubarb purée into a bowl and let it cool down until it is warm rather than hot.

3. Divide the ice cream between 2 serving bowls, pour in the rhubarb and serve immediately.

B Increase the amount of ice cream to 200 g (7 oz) between the 2 servings (this adds 50 calories)

C As for B, and have a fan wafer biscuit each as well (this adds 95 calories)

D As for B, and have 2 fan wafer biscuits each (this adds 130 calories)

Baked apple with fruit & nuts

CALORIES PER PORTION 240 kCals

A substantial, satisfying dessert that's sweet, fruity and nutty at the same time.

SERVES 1 1 large cooking apple, weighing about 200 g (7 oz) | 1 HEAPED TEASPOON SULTANAS
2 DRIED APRICOTS, CHOPPED | 1 HEAPED TEASPOON CURRANTS | 3 ALMONDS, CHOPPED
3 HAZELNUTS, CHOPPED | 1 TEASPOON DEMERARA SUGAR | 1 HEAPED TABLESPOON LOW-FAT GREEK YOGURT, TO SERVE

1. Preheat the oven to 180°C (350°F) Gas mark 4. Wash and dry the apple, then mix the sultanas, chopped apricots, currants, nuts and sugar in a small bowl. Carefully remove the apple core without cutting completely through to the very bottom, so that you leave a hollow space in the centre of the apple. Enlarge the space a little, then pack in the filling.

2. Place the apple on a piece of kitchen foil that's large enough to wrap round it completely. Pull the sides up and fold them over the top of the apple, sealing them well. Put the wrapped apple in an ovenproof dish and bake it in the preheated oven – how long this takes will depend on the size of the apple, but it should be about 45 minutes. The apple is ready if it feels tender when you squeeze it.

3. Remove the apple from the oven, carefully unwrap it and put it in a bowl. Serve with the yogurt.

B C D Use half-fat crème fraîche instead of yogurt (this adds 35 calories) and drizzle 1 teaspoon clear honey over the cooked apple (this adds 25 calories)

Warm pear compôte

CALORIES PER PORTION 200 kCals

Use firm pears rather than soft, over-ripe ones which could turn to mush when cooked.

SERVES 2 4 MEDIUM-SIZED PEARS, WEIGHING ABOUT 150 G (5 OZ) EACH | 2 TEASPOONS GRANULATED SUGAR
A FEW DROPS OF VANILLA ESSENCE | 75 G (3 OZ) LOW-FAT CRÈME FRAÎCHE OR 4 TABLESPOONS SINGLE CREAM, TO SERVE

1. Fill a saucepan with water. Peel and quarter the pears, then cut away the cores. Chop them into pieces no larger than 2 cm (just under 1 inch) and put them into the water. When all the pears are done, drain off most of the water, leaving just enough to almost cover the fruit. Add the sugar.

2. Put the pan over a medium heat, and gently bring the pears to a simmer. Cook them until they are beginning to fall apart a little, stirring regularly to make sure they don't catch. (If there seems to be a lot of water, increase the heat a little and cook some of it off; if it seems to be too dry, add a little more.) Remove the pan from the heat and add the vanilla essence. Stir the pears and put them into a bowl to cool down.

3. Once the pears are warm rather than hot, divide them into 2 serving bowls, and put the crème fraîche on the side (or drizzle the single cream over them). Serve immediately.

B Have 2 fan wafer biscuits as well (this adds 90 calories)

C Have 1 fan wafer biscuit and use 4 tablespoons double cream instead of single (this adds 135 calories)

D Have 2 fan wafer biscuits and use double cream instead of single (this adds 180 calories)

Snacks
& Treats

Snacks

Check your snacks allowance for the day from the menu plans on pages 16–17, then choose whatever you fancy from the list below.

Remember: always have a healthy snack close at hand to save you should temptation strike.

- 1 large pear (65 calories) or banana (100 calories) or orange (60 calories), or a couple of large plums (70 calories)

- A large bowlful (about 200 g/7 oz) of raspberries, cherries or strawberries (about 50 calories). Add a couple of tablespoons of low-fat Greek yogurt (75 calories in total)

- 5 celery sticks filled with 50 g (2 oz) light soft cheese (90 calories)

- 10 pitted black olives in brine, rinsed and mixed with a few chopped fresh herbs and 1 teaspoon olive oil (90 calories)

- 30 pistachio nuts in their shells (90 calories)

- 1 rye crispbread spread with 1 rounded teaspoon smooth peanut butter (110 calories) – spread the smooth side; the rough one holds almost double the quantity

- 100 g (3½ oz) reduced-fat cottage cheese with a chopped peach, nectarine or chopped slice of pineapple (about 115 calories)

- 30 g (generous 1 oz) light cream cheese with chives on 2 dark rye crispbreads, spread with (optional) Marmite (about 125 calories)

- 100 g (3½ oz) of mixed nuts toasted in Cajun spices or soy sauce. Eat no more than 20 g (¾ oz) at a time (about 125 calories). They keep well in an airtight jar

- A selection of 'crudités' – carrot sticks, cucumber batons, spring onions, strips of pepper – kept in an airtight box and used for snacking with one of the salsas on page 45 (about 130 calories)

- 10 almonds (130 calories)

- 1 apple and a 20 g (¾ oz)-piece of strong Cheddar cheese (135 calories)

- 150 g (5 oz) low-fat Greek yogurt with 50 g (2 oz) chopped fresh strawberries stirred into it (135 calories)

- 2 oatcakes spread with 20 g (¾ oz) light cream cheese with garlic and herbs (140 calories)

- 150 g (5 oz) low-fat natural yogurt with ½ teaspoon chopped seeds and 2 pieces of dried fruit, such as sunflower seeds and a couple of apricots (about 145 calories)

- 25 g (1 oz) monkey nuts (145 calories)

- 25 g (1 oz) dry-roasted peanuts 150 calories)

- A 120g can of sardines in spring water or brine – drain and rinse well – on 1 crispbread or an oatcake (about 180 calories)

- a small can of tuna in spring water, drained and mixed with 1 tablespoon extra-low-fat mayonnaise on 1 crispbread or an oatcake (about 180 calories)

- 150 g (5 oz) low-fat Greek yogurt with 3 chopped almonds scattered on it, and 1 teaspoon honey drizzled over the top (185 calories)

- Half an avocado with 1 tablespoon light mayo (205 calories)

- One of the soups on pages 82–93. They range from 90–285 calories a bowl

Treats

The difference between snacks and treats is that snacks are healthy, while treats tend to contain 'empty calories' – i.e. they have no nutritional value – but we include them in the Biggest Loser plan because they're psychologically good for you. Losing weight shouldn't be all about denial or you won't stick to it long-term – and we want you to get slim and stay slim for life.

Some people find it hard to follow any weight-loss plan that doesn't allow alcohol because their social life revolves around pubs, wine bars or clubs. Well, the good news is that you can drink on the Biggest Loser plan – so long as you don't exceed your treats allowance for the day. And if you're a chocaholic, you can use up your treats allowance on your favourite chocolate bar.

- Wine: a small 125 ml (4 fl oz) glass of red or dry white wine (85 calories); a medium 175ml (6 fl oz) glass (119 calories)

- Champagne: a small 125 ml (4 fl oz) glass (91 calories)

- Beer: a pint of lager, about 570 ml (18 fl oz) (about 163 calories); a pint of bitter (182 calories)

- Spirits: a single measure of whisky, gin or vodka (56 calories)

- Fizzy drinks: a 250 ml (8 fl oz) glass of cola (43 calories); 100 ml (3½ fl oz) tonic water (26 calories)

- Sugar added to tea or coffee has about 20 calories per teaspoonful. So if you take sugar and are on Plan A, your treats allowance won't go far

- Milk chocolate: a 32 g (generous 1 oz) snack-size Mars bar (175 calories)

- Dark chocolate: 20 g (¾ oz) or about 2 squares on most bars (110 calories)

- Crisps: a 35 g (generous 1 oz) bag of cheese and onion crisps (184 calories)

- Biscuits: 1 chocolate digestive (86 calories); 1 custard cream (57 calories)

- Cakes: 1 blueberry muffin, weighing about 54 g (generous 2 oz) (about 200 calories)

- Meringue: 1 meringue nest without cream (50 calories); with 2 tablespoons thick cream (about 150 calories)

- Ice cream: a 113 g (3 ¾ oz) scoop of vanilla (260 calories)

- Or have an extra dessert from the selection on pages 154–167. They range from 95–255 calories each.

Remember: if you're on Plan A, you have a treat allowance of 100 calories a day; Plan B – 150 calories a day; Plan C – 200 calories a day; and Plan D – 250 calories a day.

You'll find some standard calorie counts for typical treats listed on the previous page, but do read the label on your treat of choice. Find the calorie count per serving, and make sure you know what the serving size is. For example, a chocolate bar might say 220 calories per 40 g serving. If it's a 100 g bar, that means there are 2.5 servings per package, and it's up to you to work out how many squares of chocolate you can afford. You'll need to keep your wits about you!

It's important to measure the quantities of all foods you eat (apart from salad leaves without dressing) and all drinks (apart from water or black, sugarless tea and coffee), but it is absolutely VITAL that you keep a check on your treats calories. Go overboard on these and the pounds will pile back on with a vengeance …

A Final Word

Use this cookbook in whatever way is most useful to you. Mix and match meals as you like within the calorie allowance for your band. (Remember Plan A = 1,500 calories, B = 2,000 calories, C = 2,500 and D = 3,000.) Just be sure to eat a wide variety of foods so you get all the vitamins and minerals your body needs. When you've learned how to cook healthily, you'll have the tools to create meals that will help to keep you and your family slim for life.

Once you reach your target weight, be sure to celebrate. Have some 'after' photos taken by a professional photographer. Buy some flattering new clothes. Throw a big party then watch the stunned look on your friends' faces as they take in the transformation you've undergone.

Do things you were too shy to do when you felt too big. If you are single, join a dating agency. Book a beach holiday. Start training for a charity fun run. Don't be held back any longer by worrying whether people are judging you because of your weight. Now they will look at you and think, 'There's someone who looks after him-/herself.'

Whatever you do, don't slip back to the old habits that made you overweight in the first place. Continue to eat the Biggest Loser way, following the healthy eating guidelines on page 9, and you should stay slim and healthy long term.

You've achieved something amazing, which is going to affect many different areas of your life. Congratulations from all the Biggest Loser team!

Index

LOSE WEIGHT @
biggestloserclub.co.uk

What is the secret behind the success of The Biggest Loser contestants? Great trainers, healthy recipes, and The Biggest Loser Online Diet Club.

Already one of the UK's best-loved diet clubs, this scientifically proven website includes delicious menus, easy-start exercise plans, inspiring video messages from trainer Richard Callender, a world-famous food and exercise diary, and great support. The Club is 100% online so can you lose weight from the convenience of home, work or even your mobile phone.

Start today with a 7-day FREE trial. Just go to biggestloserclub.co.uk/join and enter the promotion code: **RECIPES**

biggestloserclub.co.uk